Dear Dr. Echevarria,

I send this to you as a member of Evangelicals and Catholics Together, hoping you will find it intriguing. It was quietly published on October 31st of 2017 to coincide with the 500th Anniversary of the posting of the original 95 Theses. This contemporary version is meant as an ecumenical challenge and proposition, complete with biblical defense. I believe that the term "Reunification Theology" is unique to this work, and states its ultimate goal.

I am acutely aware that the source is suspect – I am not a Doctor of Theology or Doctor of Divinity. I am not even a Doctor of Philosophy. The fact that I am a Doctor of Medicine causes many an academic to wonder what I could possibly contribute to the discussion of biblical interpretation and doctrinal truth. I can only stand by my credentials as a disciple of Christ and determined analytic. My life experiences and disposition have allowed me to consider many different denominational viewpoints with an eye to their areas of possible syncretization.

The 95Theses2017 do not claim to present some innovative or heretofore unknown explanation of Christian Doctrine. That would be foolhardy and inappropriate. They do claim to have discovered a path through the forest of trees that are historical, orthodox explanations of Christian Doctrine that has not been taken before. This path at times wanders into recognized Catholic/Orthodox territory (baptism, confession), at other times into typical Protestant territory (The Lord's Supper, The

Canon), and deep in the forest they skirt a path between the two (works and their relation to justification and salvation).

I wrote the 95Theses2017 for the rank and file Christian who is willing to consider a possible ecumenical alternative to their current denominational theology. As such, I have tried to stay away from theological jargon as much as possible and write in a simple, straightforward style, presenting arguments in a linear and transparent fashion. I also refrained from footnoting every other sentence, displaying my knowledge of which past theologian or church father has had similar ideas. The biblical exegesis presented in the text is all mine – I would be lying to attribute it to another. I stand by the justifying arguments as clear and cohesive, taking all pertinent texts into consideration.

I hope you may find the time to not only read the Theses but also the arguments written in their defense. I certainly welcome any comments or criticism. Please feel free to pass along to colleagues, or if time does not permit a personal reading, to allow a student or mentee to provide a critique. Thanks for your consideration.

Praying for Unity,

Paul

info @ 95theses2017.org

The 95Theses2017

A Biblical Defense of Reunification Theology

Semper Reformando
ad
Veritas et Unitas

Paul

Dr. Paul Dassow

Copyright © 2017 Paul Dassow, MD, MSPH

All rights reserved.

ISBN:0692958983
ISBN-13: 9780692958988

FOR ANNAMAE KOHN DASSOW (1932-2006)

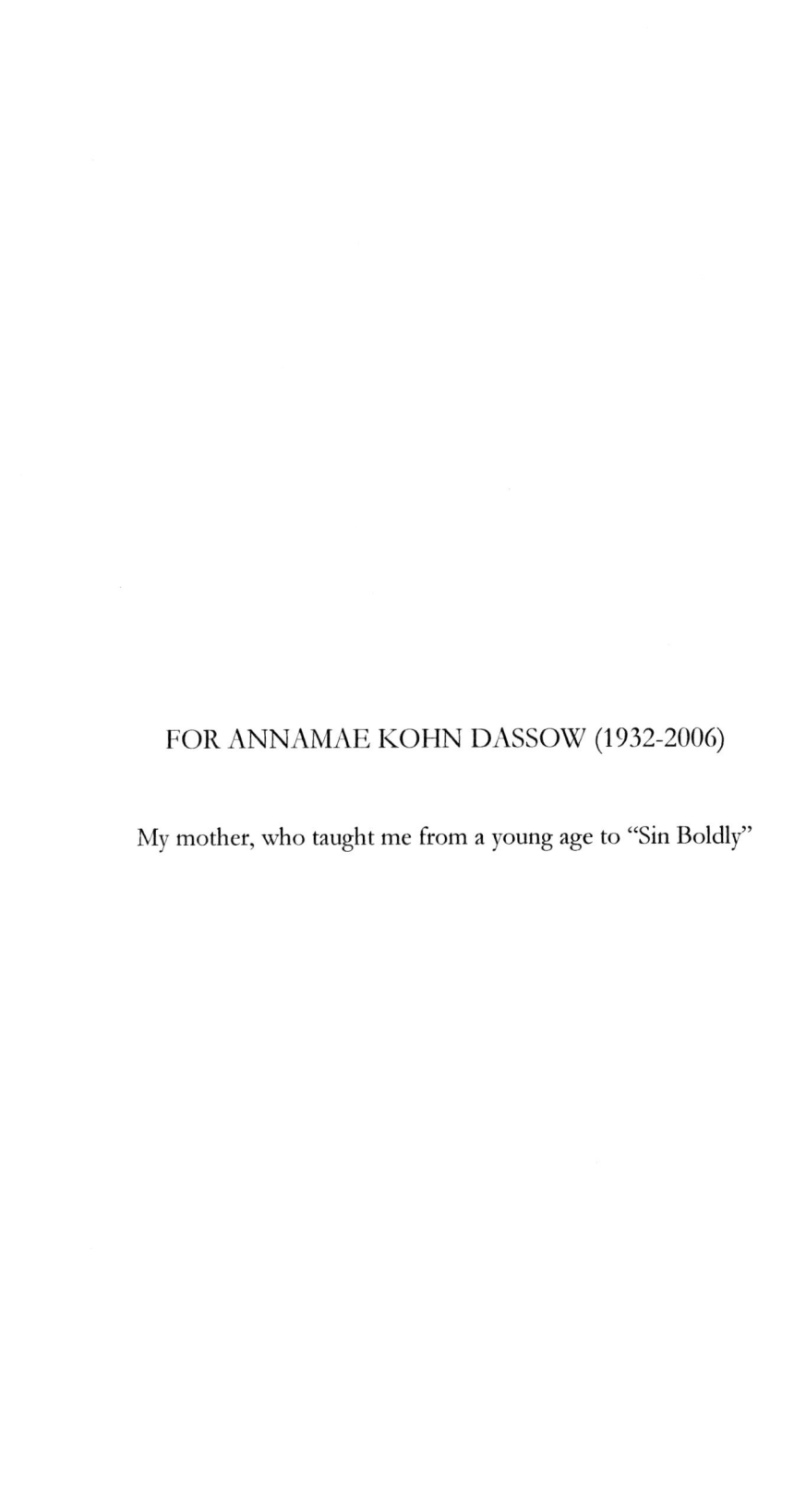

My mother, who taught me from a young age to "Sin Boldly"

CONTENTS

	Acknowledgments	i
1	Introduction	1
2	The 95Theses2017	13
3	What is Truth?	27
4	A Tale of Two Testaments	45
5	In the Beginning	65
6	Salvation	83
7	Baptism: Its Meaning	101
8	Baptism: Its Practice	127
9	The Lord's Supper	165
10	Prayer, Confession, and Forgiveness	185
11	Good Works and Holy Living	209
12	Hell and Heaven	227
13	A Roadmap to Reunification	247
	Chapter Notes	251

ACKNOWLEDGMENTS

A huge Thank You to the creators and maintainers of The Blue Letter Bible. This multi-translation, interlinear, online Bible proved immensely helpful in writing this book. I highly recommend it to anyone searching the Scriptures.

1

Introduction

What is Reunification theology?

Reunification theology is an explanation of the foundational doctrines of Christianity that adheres to the traditional, orthodox teachings of the Church, while recognizing and amending those aspects that have strayed from biblical teaching. It represents the "Middle Way." "Middle" not for the sake of compromise or "finding common ground." Rather, "Middle" because the most likely place to find God's intended meaning of a disputed doctrine is not in either extreme, but somewhere in-between. Most opposing viewpoints contain some truth. Describing the full truth takes an explanation that can incorporate the "truths" from both sides in a way that is reasonable and acceptable. Reunification theology, as summarized in the 95Theses2017, attempts to do just that.

When Martin Luther wrote the 95 Theses in 1517, he was attempting to correct errors that had crept into the Church, namely, abuses of power and corruption of the Gospel. The ensuing 500 years of reformation did indeed correct many errors. It stimulated people from all walks of life to study the Bible for themselves, and it spawned the formation and growth of countless institutions dedicated to teaching the truths of Christianity. Unfortunately, these past 500 years also witnessed

INTRODUCTION

the greatest fragmentation and polarization that the followers of Christ have experienced since the Church's inception nearly 2000 years ago. Three dominant Church sects, Orthodox, Roman Catholic, and Protestant, with the latter split into thousands of separate Protestant denominations and groups, now comprise the Body of Christ on earth.

Is this OK? Is this current state of affairs desirable, or should we be striving for a different state of being - a different worldwide witness?

I have heard many preachers and teachers defend the current status with arguments such as, "The Christian Church has been able to speak to more people in more places given all the different viewpoints and worship styles now available;" also "It is God's will that many different Christian groups exist – it will stimulate true seekers to continually return to God's Word to find out which group is teaching the real truth of Scripture."

Yet, I read something different in God's will for His Church. In Jesus' prayer for the future of His followers he earnestly pleads to His Father,

> "The Glory which You have given to Me I have given to them, that they may be one, just as We are one; I in them and You in Me, that they may be perfected in unity, so that the world may know that You sent Me, and loved them, even as You have loved Me" (Jn 17:22,23).

Perfected in unity. Certainly a lofty goal, but what would this *really* look like down here on earth with all our sinfulness, pride, and ignorance? Maybe Jesus was praying for a "spiritual" unity, the unity that some like to say already exists between all true believers in the divinity and work of Jesus; the unity that binds all Christians together in that entity called "The Invisible Church."

How convenient that our unity is invisible – no one can really judge or evaluate something that can't be seen or measured. And *"perfected in unity"* can then be one less thing to worry about or strive for – it already exists as an intrinsic characteristic of our being part of "The Invisible Church."

I think not. Although I've heard this sort of rationalization over and over, it seems more like a feeble attempt to justify our state of non-union than it is any sort of biblical defense of the Church's current state.

"So that the world may know that you sent Me."

A worldwide witness, by definition, cannot be invisible. "The world" sees and hears and experiences. That's how "the world" knows things. And if we ask "the world" if the Christian Church is perfected in unity, we will be lucky if we don't hear chuckles of laughter in response. Everyone knows the Protestants and Catholics don't get along, and the Orthodox, well, they just do their own thing and keep to themselves.

So, the time is right for a challenge to the entire Christian Church to spend considerable effort and resources to attempt the impossible – reunification under a single statement of doctrine. Reunification that shows itself in worshipping together, praying together, and working together to bring truth and light to every person and place on earth. Reunification that accepts different worship styles, different dress, and, yes, even different administrative structures. But this reunification must come with an accepted statement of the faith of the Church - a celebrated, publicized, understandable, and agreed upon statement. Anything less than that will merely perpetuate the status quo and leave the Church in its present siloed state. Anything less than that will accomplish little.

INTRODUCTION

Fair enough. But how to proceed? The 95Theses2017 were written to be a catalyst for discussion, study, and a challenge to all those who call themselves Children of God to examine their current beliefs and prayerfully consider where their current church may be mistaken in its teaching. The 95Theses2017 do not teach the doctrine of any current church on earth - they are not Orthodox or Roman Catholic or Protestant (as would be expected of a unifying statement of belief). They are critical, in one way or another, of every church. They are intended to both state the positive - what is a correct understanding of biblical teaching - and the negative - what are the common errors taught by various Christian groups. Every Christian will find much they agree with in the Theses, and something that is contrary to what they currently hold to be true.

Every person's initial and immediate response to The 95Theses2017 should be: "Who is Paul Dassow (rhymes with lasso), and why in the world does he think he can tell Christian churches around the world what is right and wrong with their theology?"

A very fair and important question. I certainly do not claim infallibility or any special revelation bestowed on me from on high. I am not a professional theologian, a writer, a narcissist looking for public affirmation of an odd Christian interpretation, or someone trying to start a new denomination. The only reason I wrote the Theses was because I felt a clear and sure call to do so. To write these and present them as I have for any other reason would be foolhardy. But that doesn't in any way speak to my credentials. Indeed. A short biography of Paul Dassow is in order.

My own descriptors, listed in approximate descending level of importance, would be: Disciple of Christ, husband, father of six, physician, professor, medical researcher, electrical engineer, home remodeler, and Masters swimmer.

I was born to Christian parents. Both were raised in orthodox Lutheran churches and my first memories of learning spiritual truths were formed in a small Missouri Synod church in the Bay Area of California in the late 60's. It was here that I earned gold stars for memorizing Scripture and it was here that I first heard a warning about other Christian churches teaching error.

About age 7, my parents decided that this particular Lutheran church was showing signs of accepting more liberal interpretations of the Bible. Sermons were becoming more topical rather than being straight explanations of biblical texts. Talk of working with other denominations, despite our doctrinal differences, crept into Sunday school discussions. And though we kids were still being taught the catechism (Luther's), it seemed like the emphasis on maintaining a pure and correct understanding of Scripture was waning. So, after some searching, the family relocated to a smaller, more conservative, more exclusive Lutheran church.

During the next 10 years I received an interesting blend of a comparative religion curriculum and an introduction to the world outside. While I was simultaneously reading the Augsburg Confession (as an early teenager) and learning how the Baptists, the Methodists and, of course, the Catholics had strayed into error, I was also mingling with an energetic, passionate group of Christians across town who believed some of the very things I was being taught were unbiblical.

Small churches have small (or nonexistent) youth groups, and our church had very little fellowship to offer my sisters and me, so my parents allowed me to attend youth group at a large, charismatic, non-denominational church where many of my friends went. These people taught that my baptism as an infant

INTRODUCTION

was quite premature and really needed to be repeated now that I was older. They taught that people choose God, not vice versa, and that the Holy Spirit's gifts should be actively practiced in daily life. They did not confess their sins every Sunday as we did, nor did they have a catechism or confession to which they doggedly adhered.

What was I to make of the contradictions?

Rather than accept or reject either one, I committed myself to understanding why and how these differences arose, and which teachings were most consistent with Scripture. I tracked down books on Early Church History, basic biblical Greek, and Arminianism. I attended a Mass with my aunt and uncle. I peppered my own pastor with questions about how we decided the Apocrypha was not fully inspired and how we are meant to resolve the apparent inconsistency between the God of Judgement in the Old Testament and the God of Love in the New. I know such activity may sound crazy for a high school student, but God made me a determined analytic, and I really wanted to figure this one out.

Large state universities have a way of expanding one's horizons and the University of Colorado was no exception. While I studied engineering, I continued to seek out opportunities to learn and experience the differences between Christians. I took part in Campus Crusade as well as Intervarsity. I found an Orthodox church in Boulder and wandered inside to see what icons were all about. I accompanied friends to Methodist and Baptist churches and listened intently trying to discern their understanding of grace and salvation. All the while, I gained a profound appreciation for how amazingly satisfied most church members were to live in isolation from their fellow believers in other denominations. The "we have it right and those other churches have it wrong" attitude that I grew up with, and questioned, was certainly not unique to my parent's church. In many denominations it ran even stronger.

It was in medical school that I officially left my parent's Lutheran church. This decision was not based on a rejection of all things Lutheran, rather it was done to show my rejection of their "Fellowship Principle." I had been transgressing this for years - fellowshipping with those outside the denomination - and it was time to make it official. It was also in medical school that I met and married by beautiful wife Jeanie. She grew up Episcopalian and was attending a Presbyterian church when we met. Two more denominations to explore and understand.

I have been blessed over the past 25 years by being able to worship with believers in Catholic, Orthodox and Protestant churches in Africa, Europe, Asia and Central America. I assure you, this has not been done with a blind eye to unscriptural practices or misleading teaching. It *has* been done in the spirit of seeking truth, and understanding the many facets of the glorious Body of Christ.

Every Christian should get to experience the gorgeous harmonies of an Anglican acapella choir in Zambia, the solemn reverence of Mass celebrated in St. Peter's Basilica, and the dignified commitment of worshippers in a Chinese house church. For these experiences I am truly grateful, and it is with these experiences and much prayerful consideration that I write the 95Theses2017. I see the fact that I am not seminary trained as a plus. I have not been so indoctrinated by one branch of Christianity that I cannot consider its other many facets.

What follows is a statement of the 95Theses2017, and their apology - that is, a reasoned explanation of their biblical validity. However, before moving forward, some words about

INTRODUCTION

hermeneutics - the "rules" of biblical interpretation.

I am convinced the most important rule in determining the meaning of a passage or phrase, and the one most often broken, is maintaining internal consistency with all other biblical texts. This is no easy task. Many passages, when taken in their most straight-forward, plain meaning will yield unworkable inconsistencies with other texts. Of course, context can help, but the greatest barrier to bringing Christians together on doctrinal understanding is the habit of focusing on certain passages over and above others that don't quite "fit" into a group's teaching on a specific subject. The correct teaching needs to "fit" all the passages that address that subject, as well as the rest of Scripture.

A quick example: First Peter 3:21 states,

> *Corresponding to that, baptism now saves you - not the removal of dirt from the flesh, but an appeal to God for a good conscience - through the resurrection of Jesus Christ.*

Really? Did we just read that? **Baptism now saves you?**

If this were the only passage I happened to read from the Bible, things would be very clear and straightforward - I get baptized and I am saved. Simple enough. I get my friends baptized and they will be saved too. Of course, this isn't the only passage that talks about the criteria for salvation, and many of those other verses talk about faith in Jesus Christ as the key element.

So what is it exactly that "saves" a person, faith in Christ or baptism? Or maybe it's not really an either/or proposition. In most of the Protestant churches I have been a part of, this passage is either ignored, because it clearly does not "fit" their "faith alone" teaching on salvation, or they quickly wave their hand in front of their face and say, "Well, that passage doesn't really mean what it says," without ever explaining why the Spirit of God prompted Peter to write such a simple, clear statement of the relation of baptism to salvation.

The correct explanation of 1 Peter 3:21 must not trample the plain meaning of the text, but it must also be consistent with all other Scripture that lays out the means of salvation. It is a task that requires careful synthesis and an open mind to explanations that we weren't taught as kids in our Sunday School class. The fact of the matter is that most Sunday School and Bible Class teachers haven't had the time or inclination to try to sort out all the differences between Christian groups, so they understandably perpetuate the party line.

The second rule of hermeneutics is a corollary to the first - Scripture needs to interpret Scripture. If a passage could have multiple meanings, or shades of meanings, and most can, then other passages need to be considered simultaneously to arrive at the correct interpretation, which will necessarily be consistent across all the passages considered.

If a church or denomination's doctrine regarding forgiveness or justification or damnation is based on 2 or 3 passages, it is likely not correct. Yes, it is certainly easier to create explanations based on 1 or 2 "proof" passages, but this will inevitably lead to error because the whole of revelation is needed to arrive at our best understanding of the truths of God's Word. This whole includes both the Old and New Testaments.

A helpful analogy in this regard is the solving of Sudoku puzzles. For those unfamiliar with solving these puzzles, suffice it to say that the numbers 1 through 9 need to be strategically placed in rows and columns in order to obtain a distinct pattern. As a puzzle is worked, it often occurs that the correct number

INTRODUCTION

entry into one of the cells could be one of 2 or 3 numerical options. Sometimes to solve the puzzle, you need to pick one of your numerical options, continue to work the puzzle, and see if the puzzle will solve. If it doesn't, you have to go back, change your original "guess" and rework the puzzle. Occasionally you have to do this multiple times to finally arrive at the correct solution.

Biblical interpretation can and should go through the same iteration. Looking back at 1 Peter 3:21, various meanings could be attached to "baptism now saves you." One would be that baptism alone is what is needed and is sufficient to obtain salvation for any person at any age. As we look at other passages, however, like John 3:16 - *"For God so loved the world that He gave His only begotten Son that whoever believes in Him should not perish but have eternal life"* - we read a different criteria for salvation: faith in Jesus. So baptism alone at any age cannot be the sole criteria for salvation. It would be inconsistent with John 3:16. But if baptism required faith in Jesus to be effective, or if baptism was the event that marked a person as coming to faith, then these two passages could be understood to be internally consistent.

There are other possible explanations of 1 Peter 3:21 in addition to the two mentioned that could also work. It would be a mistake, though, to read John 3:16 in isolation as the only criteria for salvation, just as it would be a mistake to read 1 Peter 3:21 in isolation. All passages which discuss salvation must be considered simultaneously and interpretations must be adjusted to achieve consistency. If this doesn't seem possible, then interpretations need to be changed rather than passages ignored. Unfortunately, this rarely happens in practice because people, and churches, are generally unwilling to consider that they've been wrong in their longstanding belief or teaching.

The third rule of hermeneutics is that Scripture needs to be read with an ear toward the first century Church. The Spirit of God inspired Scripture for all generations, it is true. Yet, as cultures change, as morality waxes and wanes, as dress, behaviors, and ways of life morph, we need to try to understand what Scripture meant for the first century Church. Why? Because that was the context of the writings and teachings.

Although it is possible that some Scripture was meant for later generations to fully comprehend (maybe parts of Revelation?), the words, phrases, and figures of speech were first century words, phrases, and figures of speech. It is up to us to accurately discern what these meant to our spiritual ancestors in order to not distort meaning to conform to our present circumstances. The Bible contains absolute truth. Absolute truth does not change simply because it would be convenient or comfortable for our present day. What did wearing gold jewelry mean for the first century Church? I wear gold jewelry daily on my left 4th finger but this clearly means something different than it would have 2000 years ago.

Who is this book intended for?

I did not write this book specifically for pastors, priests or academics. I certainly hope they read it and are challenged by it. Most pastors and priests have taken an oath (literally) to uphold the particular teachings of their denomination, which makes considering alternate explanations of Scripture difficult.

The person I wrote this book for is that individual who desires to understand the issues that continue to hinder unity within the Church, and what resolution may be available. Most people have given up on this – I have not.

Finally, some bookkeeping details. The source for all arguments presented in this book is the Bible, the New American

INTRODUCTION

Standard (NASB) translation, unless otherwise specified. The few other sources used are referenced at the end of this book in Chapter Notes. All Greek word definitions come from Vines unless otherwise specified. I don't consider myself an expert in biblical Greek but, thank the Lord, current online technologies allow anyone to quickly compare the original Greek words used in related Bible passages.

Each of the chapters that follow takes a group of related theses and presents a defense of the assertions contained therein. Chapters are suitable for small group study with the expectation that each chapter would take an hour to read and 30 to 60 minutes to discuss. Lastly, I will follow the convention that the word "Church," when used alone and with a capital "C," means the fellowship of all believers. It will also be capitalized when used in relation to a whole church denomination such as the Catholic Church. The word "church," used alone and with a small "c," refers to an earthly organization.

Please read, consider, look up the Bible verses on your own, pray, wrestle with the conflicts in your own understanding, discuss with your pastors and priests, and listen to the Spirit's gentle instruction. We owe it to our Lord and Savior to not only seek to understand our brothers and sisters in Christ, but also to pursue the unity He so earnestly desired.

The 95Theses2017

A Call to Christian Unity for the 21st Century Christian Church through Corporate Reformation

In 1517, a bold monk wrote 95 statements meant to correct the false teachings of the Catholic Church. He desired reformation in order to restore unity to the Body of Christ. What resulted was the beginning of the Great Fragmentation of the Church.

Today, 5 centuries later, the Church has fractured to the point of becoming undefinable. Over 10,000 separate denominations exist, each with its own teaching, worship style, and governance. The current Church is clearly not what Jesus intended when he prayed, *"The glory which You have given Me I have given to them, that they may be one, just as We are one; I in them and You in Me, that they may be perfected in unity, so that the world may know that you sent Me, and loved them, even as You have loved Me."* (John 17:22,23)

The following 95 statements were written to challenge every 21st century Christian, and Christian church, to begin the process of coalescing around a common understanding of Christian doctrine for the purpose of becoming perfected in unity.

Soli Deo Gloria

… THE 95THESES2017

1. The definitive revelation of God to humans (The Canon) is contained in the 39 books of the Hebrew Bible, The Tenakh, along with the 27 books, written after the death of Jesus, that were identified as the inspired Word of God by the Ecumenical Councils.

2. The words, phrases, and figures of speech used in the original languages in The Canon were expressly intended by the Spirit of God to communicate an accurate and balanced understanding of the character of God and His intentions for His creation.

3. Translation of The Canon into contemporary languages can introduce error and thus must be done with great care to insure the most accurate rendering of the original words, phrases, and figures of speech.

4. Any apparent conflicts within the text of The Canon can be resolved through appropriate interpretation.

5. Those Christian groups that teach that The Canon contains spiritual truths alongside error, or uninspired text, are at risk of propagating misunderstanding and creating a new religion incompatible with Christianity.

6. Although there are clearly other historical and contemporary writings that contain thoughts, ideas, and instruction that were inspired by the Spirit of God, they should not be used to form the basis of Christian doctrine.

7. Writings consistent with the teaching of The Canon that have inspired various Christian groups towards a God pleasing life, and have been used as a source of enlightenment, need to be viewed as secondary and subservient to The Canon.

8. Writings used by those who self-identify as Christians, which contain teachings that contradict The Canon, are not inspired by the Spirit of God.

9. Those groups that are guided by such writings need to be confronted with these contradictions with the intention of persuading them to abandon these uninspired writings.

10. The Canon exists in two portions: that delivered to humanity prior to the incarnation of the Messiah, commonly referred to as the Old Testament, and that delivered after the incarnation, commonly referred to as the New Testament.

11. The Old Testament describes God's creation of the Universe, the establishment of His law and justice for humanity, and His plan for the redemption of a rebellious human race.

12. The New Testament focuses on the mercy of God made manifest in the life and redemptive work of Jesus of Nazareth and His instructions to His followers in light of this completed work.

13. These two portions represent the continuous and complementary revelation of the Spirit of God to humanity and all Christian teaching needs to be consistent with its content.

14. The New Testament is in no way better or more accurate than the Old Testament, rather it completes the full revelation of God.

15. The New Testament does add information to the Old Testament which serves to reveal His intentions for creation in light of the coming of the Messiah.

16. As a result of the additional revelation contained in the New Testament, some practices of those earnestly seeking to follow God's desires have been altered to reflect the fulfilment of God's redemptive plan.

17. In particular, the use of sacrifices to atone for sin has been ended and the recommended earthly consequences for sin have been modified.

18. The moral absolutes of God, initially described in the Old Testament, have not changed throughout the ages.

19. These moral absolutes continue to include prohibitions against idolatry, adultery, murder, greed, fornication, theft, and homosexuality.

20. Those persons or groups that teach that God has changed his moral absolutes over time do so to soothe their consciences and the consciences of others, to the harm of everyone.

21. God created all matter and energy from nothing.

22. God created a wide variety of living organisms in an orderly, sequential fashion as described in the first chapter of Genesis, and reflected in the fossil record of the earth.

23. Those Christians or Christian groups that insist that the period of God's creative activity was limited to 144 earth-hours misinterpret the language of Genesis 1 and dismiss the veracity of the earth's fossil record.

24. The creation of life over a significantly longer period than 144 earth-hours in no way invalidates God's existence, His preeminence, or His promises.

25. All organisms were given the ability to adapt to changes in their environments, including the ability to acquire DNA from other organisms.

26. All changes to DNA that added new information, resulting in changes to the structure and function of an organism, were designed and implemented by God.

27. Human beings represent God's final creative act and are distinctly different from all other living creatures in that they are imbued with the image of God.

28. This special imprint of God on humans is reflected in their ability to understand God's creative work in the universe; to experience joy, guilt, humor and creativity; and to be morally responsible for choices they make.

29. The first humans freely chose to disobey God thus bringing condemnation and destruction upon themselves and their descendants.

30. In order to heal the severed relationship with God, and to satisfy God's perfect justice and perfect love, God designed a pathway to save humans from eternal destruction.

31. This pathway necessitated the living of a perfect life and the sacrificial death of a person capable of bearing the cumulative moral failure of all humanity.

32. This person, the Christ, the Messiah, who was promised to our first human ancestors, was Jesus of Nazareth, a man fully human and fully divine.

33. Although the coexistence of full humanity and full divinity in a single person is difficult to understand, this union was God's perfect solution for enabling human restoration.

34. Those persons or groups that teach that Jesus was not fully human and fully divine are not Christian.

35. Those persons or groups that teach that Jesus was a creation of God, or that he is not an integral part of a singular God, or that there are multiple Gods in the universe, do not understand who Jesus is and thus distort the truths of Christianity.

36. The gift of eternal life, made possible by the life and death of Jesus of Nazareth, is given to all humans who have been adopted into the Family of God.

37. This adoption is granted to all baptized adults who fully believe and trust in God and the promises of God; it is also offered to their young children.

38. Prior to Jesus' birth, this belief and trust included God's work of creation, His provision for covering the sin of humanity through participating in various sacrifices and rituals, and the promise of a Messiah who would bring a New Covenant from God.

39. Since Jesus' life, death, and resurrection, this belief and trust must now include accepting Jesus as Lord and Savior, the promised Messiah whose death was the necessary and final sacrifice to atone for human disobedience.

40. Apostasy, that is, losing one's belief in God and the promises of God, can occur and results in breaking the familial relationship between God and the unbelieving person.

41. Those persons or groups that teach that belief and trust in Jesus as Lord and Savior are not necessary for eternal life are not Christian, are not part of the family of God, and are

guilty of leading others into eternal destruction.

42. Baptism into the name of the Father, and of the son, and of the Holy Spirit, is the usual and expected event marking the union of a person with the Body of Christ.

43. Baptism results in forgiveness of sins, a change in the relationship between God and the baptized person, and the promise that the Spirit of God will come and live in the heart of the baptized person.

44. Those persons or groups that teach that baptism is merely symbolic and that no significant spiritual changes occur during baptism fail to recognize the importance of this event in the life of those becoming followers of Jesus.

45. Baptism in no way guarantees eternal life; the relationship established between God and the person baptized can be severed by unbelief in God or the promises of God.

46. The baptism of young children and infants is an appropriate activity based on their need of Christ's righteousness, and God's demonstrated desire to bless them and accept them as Children of God.

47. Those Christian groups that teach against the baptizing of young children and infants needlessly deny them the benefits of baptism and fail to comprehend either their need for forgiveness and/or God's provision for the children of believers.

48. It is not known at what age the children of believers are judged by God based on their personal faith; this age is likely different for every person.

49. The fate of young children and infants of adult believers who die without having been baptized is not known, however, God is just and merciful and He honors the intent of His children.

50. Likewise, the fate of those persons who die in the womb is not known, but God promises His judgments will be righteous.

51. The Church, also known as the Body of Christ, and the Family of God, consists of those believers who have been baptized into Christ, along with their baptized infants and young children.

52. All members of the Church are given the right to be called Children of God; those who use this title for all humans use it inaccurately and lead non-Church members into thinking they are part of the Family of God when they are not.

53. The life of a Christian will be marked by a striving for obedience, love towards others, and evangelism.

54. Good works, and works of faith, are necessary activities that complete our faith.

55. Good works in no way earn or merit our salvation; yet, good works are so intertwined with faith that we will be judged by our works when Christ returns.

56. Those persons whose lives are dominated by sinful behaviors and activities demonstrate that they are not a part of the Body of Christ, no matter what verbal statements they may make.

57. The Lord's Supper, alternately known as Holy Communion and the Eucharist, is a celebration and remembrance of the

life and death of Jesus.

58. This celebration and remembrance should be cherished and practiced by all Children of God old enough to understand its significance and meaning.

59. The Lord's Supper is not a sacrifice, although it is a memorial to Jesus' ultimate sacrifice for us on the cross.

60. The elements of the Lord's Supper, typically bread and wine, represent the body and blood of Jesus and are ingested as nourishment for both our body and soul.

61. Although the bread and the wine are never physically transformed into the body and blood of Jesus, the latter become truly present for believers, nourishing their souls and strengthening their union with Christ.

62. Those persons participating in The Lord's Supper who do not understand the spiritual significance of this celebration or who participate with unrepentant sin, do harm to themselves.

63. Those Christian groups that teach that The Lord's Supper is purely symbolic and that real spiritual food is not received by faithful participants, fail to understand the glorious provision God intends for His Children through this memorial meal.

64. The ideal frequency for celebrating The Lord's Supper is not known, but given the blessings bestowed on each participant, the Church should actively seek opportunities to celebrate this meal when gathered together.

65. Prayer is a precious gift given to the Children of God whereby they can directly communicate with God,

expressing their love, worship, and requests.

66. Each and every Christian should engage in prayer as a daily discipline.

67. All prayer should be addressed to God – either the Father, Son, or Holy Spirit.

68. No prayers should be addressed to humans, including Jesus' mother Mary or other Saints, as this naturally leads to the appearance of deification, fosters confusion regarding the role of Christ as mediator between God the Father and man, and does not conform to the instruction of Jesus regarding prayer.

69. All Children of God are expected to practice confession of their sins.

70. Confession of sins with a repentant heart results in forgiveness of these sins.

71. The forgiveness of sins granted to Children of God by faith through participation in confession, baptism, and prayer, is real, complete, and effective.

72. Those sins that remain unconfessed, or are not specifically addressed through prayer, will be covered by the righteousness of Christ at the Final Judgement .

73. Those persons and groups that teach that all of a person's sins, including all past, present and future sins, are forgiven at the moment a person comes to faith in Christ, fail to recognize God's glorious provision for ongoing spiritual cleansing throughout a Christian's life.

74. This recurrent spiritual cleansing refreshes, rejuvenates, and energizes His Children, allowing them to live free from guilt and the encumbrances of sin.

75. Sanctification, or being made holy, is a work of the Holy Spirit which involves deepening our daily commitment to live sacrificially for Christ.

76. Although the Spirit's work enables us to resist sin, no person is able to fully submit, fully obey, or fully perform those works desired by God.

77. Thus, sanctification is a process that is complete only after we are fundamentally changed by God after death.

78. Those persons or groups that teach that a sinless life is possible prior to death are in error and risk leading people into an overinflated view of themselves, or a state of frustration at not being able to achieve this end.

79. Those groups that teach that humans become Gods, or essentially equivalent to God, in this life or in the life to come, fail to acknowledge that God's intention was to bring certain humans into His family as adopted members, never to elevate them to being equal to Himself.

80. Every person who dies as a member of the Body of Christ will be granted eternal life.

81. This eternal life will be lived in communion with God the Father, Jesus Christ, and the Holy Spirit on a recreated and perfect earth.

82. Every person granted eternal life will be in the care of God the Father after death and will experience His perfect love and comfort.

83. No Child of God will experience punishment, abandonment, or a requirement of penance after death.

84. Those Christian groups that teach a period of penance after death for Children of God do great damage to, and minimize the gift of, salvation earned by Jesus on the Cross.

85. This teaching also fosters fear and an apprehension for dying which directly contradicts the comforting words of Jesus to those he came to save.

86. The number of those being granted eternal life is known only to God and was known to God before the creation of the universe.

87. Those groups who say only a specific, known number will be granted eternal life fail to recognize symbolic language in prophetic biblical texts.

88. The day of Christ's return to earth to bring His judgment upon all humanity, both dead and alive, is known only to God the Father.

89. Any person who says they know the day of Christ's coming is mistaken and does damage to the Church through spreading false information masquerading as prophesy.

90. Not all humans will be saved; there will not be a second chance for repentance and turning to Jesus as Lord and Savior after death.

91. Those persons or groups that teach that all humans will eventually be granted eternal life are spreading false hope to those who are actually headed for eternal destruction.

92. Those persons who die outside of the Body of Christ will experience a period of Divine judgment consisting of abandonment and severe anguish of the soul and spirit prior to undergoing eternal destruction.

93. Eternal destruction will consist of annihilation of soul and spirit that will be never ending and irreversible.

94. Those persons or Christian groups that teach that God will subject those condemned to never-ending physical and psychological torment malign the character of God.

95. There is clear and abundant scriptural teaching that the final fate of those who are condemned is not eternal life, albeit, a wretched life, but rather death, both permanent and complete.

THE 95THESES2017

3

What is Truth?

Suppose I told you that the book you are currently holding is actually made up of about 10^{24} tiny particles all stuck together. That's the number 1 followed by 24 zeros, or 10 trillion trillion particles! What if I also told you that each of these particles, let's call them "atoms", wasn't just a solid chunk, but was really like a tiny solar system with specks of energy zipping around a central core at roughly 5 million miles per hour. All this activity, going on in your hands, right now. Would you believe me?

I expect that you would. Even though you cannot see these tiny particles, or feel the specks of energy moving, or *in any way experience or confirm, using your senses, the existence of such "atoms,"* I still think you would believe me. If I asked if anyone was willing to risk his or her life over the truth of my assertion that this book is made up of these particles, I expect many people would - maybe even a large majority.

Why? Why do so many people strongly believe in something they cannot see or hear or touch or experience in any way? The reason is that people have heard this explanation of what matter is made of from some source they think is credible. Believable. Trustworthy. That source was likely either a textbook or a teacher. These sources define truth for us. In the case of the textbook, we trust that someone, or maybe a group of people, performed some kind of scientific experiment that led to the inescapable conclusion that atoms do indeed exist, and that all those things that are not pure energy are made from a bunch of these atoms.

What if you found out that only one person in history made the claim that all matter is made up of atoms. This person said they did some experiments, maybe even wrote down how they did them, and published their findings in a science journal. Would you believe it then? That would make the truth of the claim a bit more questionable. We tend to believe science, that is, human reason interpreting and making sense of well-designed experiments, but trusting what one person says is dodgy. People sometimes don't see things clearly, or they misinterpret what they are seeing, or sometimes they just flat lie. We would hope that a textbook, or teacher, would not present something as truth unless many people have come to the same conclusion after independently examining the evidence.

How do we decide about the truth of historical events? Did George Washington ever cut down one of his father's cherry trees?

This story, made famous by a biographer named Mason Locke Weems, started to circulate in the early 1800's. As told by Weems, George Washington received a hatchet when he was about 6 years old. He was delighted with the gift and was soon out whacking most everything he could find. When he came upon a young cherry tree in the family garden, he took his axe to the bark, which ended up causing the tree to die. Sometime later George's father noticed that one of his favorite trees had died due to being "barked." He came into the house and angrily asked young George if he knew who might have done the deed. George, taken aback, is said to have paused, but then quickly recovered his wits and confessed, "I cannot tell a lie, father, you know I cannot tell a lie! I did cut it with my little hatchet." George's father's anger quickly melted away and as he took George into his arms he said, "My son, that you should not be afraid to tell the truth is more to me than a thousand trees!" Mr. Weems reported that he obtained this story from an elderly neighbor of the Washington family.[1]

So, did this event really happen or not? Was it an accurate retelling of history by someone who was there, or heard about it firsthand, or merely a made up story to glorify an already greatly esteemed leader?

Most historians have concluded this is a completely fictitious story.[2] But on what basis? It is true that the story came to us from a single source. That, in and of itself, does not mean the story is not true, but since there were not a handful of eyewitnesses each agreeing with the facts at hand, we should be cautious in our acceptance of the story as truth. We should consider Mr. Weem's motives for sharing the story. Was he most concerned about historical accuracy? Did he have a history of truth-telling himself, or was he prone to exaggeration? Did Mr. Weems have anything to be gained by telling this story? (As author of the biography, he definitely had an interest in selling books)

Another important aspect to consider is the content of the story itself. Are the facts reasonable? Although giving a 6-year-old a hatchet for a gift would probably not be considered appropriate in this day and age, in the mid 1700's in rural Virginia, it probably was. If the story had told of little George cutting clear through the trunk of the young tree with one great swing, most people would smell a tall tale. There was no such mention of great childhood strength. George is said to have injured the bark of the tree which later led to its demise. Both of these details are quite reasonable. As far as the interaction

WHAT IS TRUTH

between George and his father is concerned, the bold childhood confession and the paternal response may be uncommon, but certainly not unheard of. This event could have happened. Whether or not it actually did will forever remain unknown.

Trying to determine the truth about young George Washington's antics is one thing. Trying to determine the truth of writings that claim to be the Word of God is quite another.

The existence of at least one very powerful and very intelligent being is quite apparent to anyone who is willing to consider the facts of the universe. The complexity of function of just one human biologic system shouts intelligent design.

As a physician, I get to see this every day in my clinic. The human brain contains roughly 100 billion nerve cells called neurons. Each of these neurons connects to and communicates with about 10 thousand of its neighbors in a highly orchestrated fashion. That's 100 trillion chemical connections inside every person's brain! That's what it takes to make us walk, talk, hear, see, and reason. Any person who uses their 100 trillion connections to think that all these connections came about by the random association of atoms isn't thinking clearly. All science, and all human experience, suggests otherwise.[3]

There are two possibilities when it comes to communication between the One responsible for our existence and ourselves. Either this creator, which I will call God, designed and built us humans and has chosen to not communicate with us, or He (using the traditional pronoun for God) has chosen to communicate with us in some meaningful way. Given that He created us with the natural ability to learn languages, to speak, and to communicate abstract and detailed ideas amongst ourselves, it is hard to imagine that He would desire no communication with us - the very beings to whom He gave these abilities. He also made us with a strong desire to know why we are here. What is our purpose? Humans throughout the ages and in all cultures have struggled with these questions, desperately seeking an answer. Some have hypothesized that God has left us alone to answer these questions for ourselves; that the way we live out our lives determines the meaning of our existence. Maybe. However, if that were the case, then the answer to our purpose would always be pure conjecture. Right and wrong would necessarily be a matter of opinion, leading to the awful realization that calling mass murders such as the holocaust a heinous crime would just be someone's opinion.

No, it makes more sense that a God who created beings who have an innate sense of morality, who desire to know why they exist, and who are able to communicate and understand abstract ideas, would give these beings some guidance. But how? How would God communicate with us if He chose to do it? He certainly could take on some physical form and appear to one or many of us and just speak. He could place thoughts in each and every human's mind at some time in their life, or every day. He could cause us to hear His voice, either by creating soundwaves for us or by just stimulating that part of our brain that interprets incoming sound. He could have created a book in some discoverable language that He left for everyone to read. At various times in human history, claims that God has spoken to humanity in each of these ways have surfaced. How is anyone to know which of these claims is true, if any?

The criteria used for deciding whether a report of a divine communication is true or not has some similarities to deciding if George chopped down that cherry tree. First of all, does the content make sense? What do we think God would want to communicate to us? Most of us would hope He would answer the 2 big questions, why are we here and what is our purpose. He might give us some information about Himself. Giving us a set of rules and/or expectations would be very helpful. Telling us about our history would also give us some sense of where we as humans have been and where we might he going.

Purported communications that contain obvious inaccuracies would be immediately suspect. If someone claimed they had heard from God and He said the earth is really flat after all, we probably don't need to listen to much else. If a supposed divinely provided text states there are humans living on the moon, or that people can naturally read someone else's mind, then that text contains obvious error and wouldn't be thought to come from God.

What shouldn't be excluded are reports of supernatural activities. God's creation of the universe, and of us, was a feat no human could dream about. It would be expected that a revelation from God might include stories of supernatural events and unexplainable happenings. If God created everything we see, He can certainly manipulate it in any manner He might choose. It is incredibly inconsistent to hear so-called literary "critics" determine that a story is mere myth because it includes supernatural events. The critic's own existence is a supernatural event! I would doubt a history of the universe was from God if it *didn't* include some details about how God had supernaturally intervened in that history.

The content should also tell us things that we otherwise wouldn't know. God could communicate the obvious to us - sex is required to procreate, the earth takes 365 days to travel around the sun, life expectancy is around 80 years. These things are indeed true, but why would God bother to tell us what we can figure out on our own. The purpose of any communication would be specifically to tell us those things we couldn't know without being told. How did the universe come to be? What is the origin of evil? Is there any existence after we die? Those questions can only be answered by God. If the content also included forecasts or predictions of future events that came true, that would be a remarkable indicator of divine authorship. One prediction coming true could be just plain luck, but 2, 3 or more would be strong evidence of a truth claim.

The method that the information is made known to us and who brings it would be quite important. We noted in the story of the cherry tree that having a single person bring a report, without any witnesses or corroborators, does not engender much confidence in its truth. It could be true, but having 3 or 4 or 5 people who witnessed the same event or heard the same story or were somehow given the same information makes a truth claim much more likely. If a person, or persons, say they are bringing the very words of God to the rest of us, what motive might they have to stretch the truth, or even make things up. Are they expecting financial benefit or fame or power for their efforts? Such considerations need to be explored before a reasonable judgement can be made.

About 400 years before Jesus of Nazareth was born, a group of books, 24 in all, were identified by a group of middle eastern spiritual leaders as God's revelation to humans. These books were written by at least 27 different people over a period of about 1 thousand years. These books included a story of how the universe was created. They included a description of the origin of evil. They included a detailed list of rules and expectations for human behavior. They included colorful stories of God's interactions with a particular human family and their descendants. They included predictions of future events, some in cryptic visionary language and others with detailed names and places. There is no single text, or group of texts, like it anywhere in the world. But, is the claim true? Is this the communication from God that we might expect?

In terms of content, as noted above, it is part history book, part rule book, part worship manual, and part human critique. Its story of the creation of all things tells of the sudden appearance of matter and energy followed by the sequential formation of stars, planets, and life, the latter progressing from plants to fish to birds to mammals, and finally to humans. This account was written over 3000 years ago, long before any science might help the author know how this happened. Its account exactly matches what we now know about the formation of the universe. This is unlikely a lucky guess.

There is much content describing historical events, places, and people. Although much of it is hard to verify, nothing has been found in any of the books that contradicts known facts. Archeologists and anthropologists have actually used many of the books to find ancient cities and battlegrounds.[4] Dates given in the text that were once thought to be inaccurate, have been proven correct.[5] Descriptions of supernatural interventions into human affairs such as the toppling of the walls of Jericho are supported by the archeological findings.[6] The descriptions of a worldwide flood also have significant geological evidence.[7]

There is nothing in the content of these books that would disqualify them from being considered a communication from God. This is not to say that the books are all easy to understand or that there is nothing controversial in them.

In the first book, God refers to Himself in the plural, *"let Us make man in Our image"* (Gen 1:26), while in the last book it is stated, *"Has not one God created us"* (Mal 2:10)? Overt miracles such as the lengthening of a day and the granting of a human voice to a donkey challenge our notion of what is possible. The sections on law lay down strict penalties including death for adultery and homosexuality. Many today consider these penalties too harsh and reason that the God who made humans wouldn't pronounce such judgements. Opinions aside, however, none of these sections of text provide objective arguments against God being behind their creation.

Running through all 24 books are themes of rebellion, judgement, atonement through the shedding of blood, and God's sovereignty. Some books emphasize one theme more than another, but they all contain at least hints of each. Lurking in the shadows, and in the symbolism built into the law, is the promise of a redeemer - one who will come to free people from their bondage to sin (disobedience) and its corresponding judgement.

Remember that these books were written by at least 27 different people over a period of 1 thousand years! Just the fact that they present a cohesive, uniform picture of God is remarkable. Imagine a different person writing a book every 40 years, each telling a part of a single story, over the period 1000 to 2000 AD. The authors refer to each other's works, describe God's interactions with the people in their own time period, and, despite living in different centuries, present consistent accounts of God's character, God's expectations, God's promises, and God's judgements. This suggests a supernatural origin.

These 24 books became known as the Hebrew Bible since the many writers were all descendants of Abraham, Isaac, and Jacob. These same 24 books, rearranged into 39 books, make up the Old Testament in Christian Bibles.

The New Testament of the Christian Bible has a strikingly similar history. Consisting of 27 books written by 9 different authors over a period of 40 some years, it continues the story contained in the Hebrew Bible. Specifically, it focuses on the arrival and teaching of the One promised to rescue the human race from judgement. It is important to note the many specific predictions contained in the Old Testament that this person,

Jesus of Nazareth, fulfilled. He was born in Bethlehem (Mic 5:2). He was born to a virgin (Is 7:14). He was a direct descendent of King David (2 Sam 7:12-16). He spent his early years in Egypt (Hos 11:1). He was called the Son of God (Ps 2:1-12). He was called the Prince of Peace (Is 9:6,7). He performed healings (Is 35:5,6). He was hailed by the people as a king riding on a colt (Zech 9:9). He was betrayed for 30 pieces of silver (Zech 11:12,13). He was executed by being lifted up on a tree (Num 21:6-9). During His execution He would be given gall and vinegar to drink (Ps 69:21). He would not have any of his bones broken (Ps 34:19,20). He would rise from the dead (Ps 16:8-11). He would do all this willingly without putting up a fight (Gen 22:1-18).

These predictions of a future Rescuer do not appear in just one of these books, in one paragraph entitled, "Prophesies of the coming Messiah." On the contrary, these predictions appear in many of the books, scattered about, tucked away among the history and the law. As a reader comes upon these clues, it becomes apparent that the writers themselves were likely unaware that they were penning prophecy. The telltale phrases "My Son," or "My Servant," or "the lamb" signal a reference to someone outside of the writer's experience. This was not a humanly orchestrated literary event.

Jesus was born about 450 years after the last book of the Hebrew Bible was written. Most books that are written are forgotten after about 50 years (some long before that). Imagine what it would have taken for Jesus to purposefully fulfil all of these prophesies.

First, he would need to know them all. Then He would have needed to recognize that His Bethlehem birth fit the prophecy. His parents would need to have the proper ancestry. He would need to somehow spread the word that His mom was a virgin when He was born. He would need to get his parents to take Him to Egypt for a couple of years when he was a toddler. Next, He would need to learn how to perform healings. He would need to get the people to call Him the Son of God and Prince of Peace. He would need to find a colt to ride on into Jerusalem when the time was right. He would need to arrange the betrayal price for His life between the Chief priests and Judas. He would need to orchestrate His death so that He was crucified, and that after He died, His legs would not be broken, as was the custom of the Romans. Finally, He would need to stage a resurrection that was so air-tight that a body was never found, and he would need to insure that many people would report His reappearance as a living being.

All this was not humanly possible.

The arrival of Jesus as the promised Messiah, fulfilling numerous prophesies scattered throughout the Old Testament books, provides strong evidence that these writings are from God. It also supports the claim that the books of the New Testament are a continuation of the Old. There are at least another 100 predictions in the Old Testament that have strong historical evidence of coming to pass just as predicted.[8] This goes way beyond any purely human explanation. Our reason, and mathematical analyses, tells us that such accurate prophesying is not possible without supernatural knowledge.

But what about other books, other texts, that have claimed to be revelations from God? How did the Great Assembly of leaders (as they were called) in the fifth century BC decide on the 24 books in the Hebrew Bible, and how did the 27 books of the New Testament make the cut?

In one sense, the answer to the question of "How" doesn't really matter. What if I asked the question, "How was the Grand

Canyon formed?" I could probably find many theories about earthquakes or floods or tectonic plate movements or slow steady erosion over millions of years. One or more of these explanations would probably be correct. Does it matter? For the sake of geological knowledge it would be nice to know. But, the Canyon is there in all its glory, no matter how it came to be. So too is the Bible.

Still, we humans, especially those who are looking for reasons to doubt the Bible's claims, want to know details. What did the Great Assembly talk about when they met to decide which books were inspired by God? What criteria did they use? Did they consider other texts? Was there full agreement or were there contentious debates? Did they vote? The same questions could be asked of the people who decided on the 27 books of the New Testament, in addition to: Why wasn't the Gospel of Thomas included? Since the author of Hebrews is unknown, how could it be considered alongside the Apostle Paul's work? Why didn't they include any books written in the first 10 years after Jesus' resurrection?

The answers to most of these questions are just unknown. However, from a practical point of view, if God did indeed choose to communicate with humanity, it makes sense that He would insure that His words reached us in a way that were discoverable, understandable, and free from corruption. Why would He tolerate gibberish or error? He is God. He created all things. He could certainly cause 36 or so people to write down exactly those words He wanted to convey and then have these various works bundled together in a single communication that we humans rightly recognize as divinely inspired. The criteria that were used to include the 66 books of the Bible were the criteria that God chose. To think otherwise would be to say that God couldn't manage to get the right words in the right books He wanted us to have. That's irrational.

There are, of course, other books that claim to be divinely inspired. Maybe there is supposed to be more than 1 group of books. Maybe we are supposed to recognize a volume 2, or an addendum to the Bible. The three problems with extra-biblical books that claim to be additional or amended words from God are that (1) they are all written by single authors without others to corroborate their content; (2) they bring messages that conflict with the current Bible; and (3) they lack the supernatural characteristic of fulfilled prophecy.

The Book of Mormon, for example, published by Joseph Smith in 1830, is the purported story of the Nephites and Lamanites, lost tribes of Israel, who lived in the United States after the resurrection of Christ. Despite Book of Mormon reports of large cities and large battles, absolutely no evidence has been found to substantiate any of the accounts. The book contains no fulfilled prophecies. There is wide consensus among those who study the Bible that the presentation of Jesus in the Book of Mormon, and its message of merit-based salvation, is inconsistent with that taught in the 66 books of the Bible.

The Koran, written by the single author Muhammad sometime in the early seventh century, is claimed to be the Word of God communicated to Muhammad by the angel Gabriel. It teaches about the one God Allah, while also providing guidance about proper human conduct, what constitutes a just society, and principles of an equitable economic system. Like the Book of Mormon, it contains no specific prophesies of times or places that have been fulfilled. Like the Book of Mormon, it teaches a different Jesus than does the Bible. The Koran specifically denies the divinity of Christ, denies that He is the Son of God, and denies His crucifixion on a Roman cross. The Koran also presents a merit-based salvation, which, it is interesting to note, is the basis of all religions other than that revealed in the Bible.

What about the Apocrypha? Most of these 15 or so books were written after the last book of the Hebrew Bible, Malachi, and before the birth of Jesus. Should these books be part of the Canon - that is, the books intended by God to be the definitive reference for life? Should they be considered the inerrant Word of God, along with the other 66 books of the Bible?

The Apocryphal books were never considered part of the Hebrew Bible and have never been considered part of the New Testament. The question of which, if any, are meant to be part of the Canon has been a point of contention throughout the church's history.

The Catholic Church considers 11 of these books to be deuterocanonical, or "the second canon." As such, they consider them to be fully inspired Words of God, equal in authority to the rest of the Bible. The latest official statement about these books being part of the Canon came in 1546 at the Council of Trent. The reason for this restatement was to counteract the growing sentiment among the Protestant reformers that they should not be considered on equal par with the protocanon, or "first Canon." Early church theologians were split on the issue. St. Jerome (405) was against their inclusion, but St. Augustine (397) argued in favor of them. St. Athanasius thought the Book of Baruch and the Letter of Jeremiah should be included, but not 7 of the other writings. Two early Councils, one in Hippo (393) and another in Carthage (397), listed them as part of the Bible.

For those not acquainted with these disputed texts, it is important to know something about them. Five of these "books" represent text added onto existing Hebrew writings. The Story of Susanna was appended as Daniel 13; The Idol, Bel and the Dragon as Daniel 14; The Song of the Three Children as Daniel 3:24-90; The Prayer of Manassas was added to the end of 2nd Chronicles; and the Rest of Esther was added as Chapters 10:4 to

16:24 to the book by the same name. Four of the books are histories of the Jewish people during the period 400 to 100 BC.

All teachers of the Christian faith would agree that these books are important historical writings, worthy of our reading and consideration. There are, however, some simple and compelling reasons to exclude them from the Canon.

First, some of these books contain obvious historical error. Judith 1:1 opens, "It was the twelfth year of the reign of Nebuchadnezzar, who ruled over the Assyrians in the great city of Nineveh." Accepted history tells us Nebuchadnezzar ruled the Babylonians from Babylon. The book of Tobit says that he [Tobit] was alive during the revolt of Jeroboam in 931 BC and also during the Assyrian capture of Israel in 721 BC. This 200+ year lifespan directly contradicts his stated age at death of 112 years (Tobit 14).

Second, the fact that many of these "books" were actually short stories, composed by anonymous Greek authors, tacked onto existing Hebrew prophetic writings, creates a sense of inauthenticity. Third, Jesus and His apostles quote from nearly every book in the Hebrew Bible, calling it "Scripture." They never once quote from any of the Apocryphal books. Fourth, all Christians accept the 66 books of the Hebrew Bible and the New Testament as the Word of God. Only about half the Church accepts the deuterocanonical books. Harking back to the argument that God would provide to humans a communication that is discoverable, it follows that the Church, His Church, would be given the insight to identify it. The Church is unanimous in its recognition of the Old Testament, sans Apocryphal books, and the New Testament as fully inspired and authoritative. These books define truth.

Two other important questions relating to the veracity of the

Bible need to be considered: (1) Why did God wait so long to provide humanity with His definitive instructions about life's meaning, its purpose, and its ultimate destiny; and (2), If God really wanted to have a relationship with all humans, why doesn't He just show Himself to every person in some tangible way?

In terms of the timing of the writing of the Bible, God could have written down His law and His expectations for human behavior at the time He created Adam and Eve. This could then have been passed down to all their descendants so that all would have the benefit of this knowledge, free from the typical error introduced by verbally passing information down from generation to generation. God chose not to do this. Instead, God gave the first humans the gift of language and speech, but not a written language. He allowed them to develop this on their own. Our best historical research indicates that we humans did not develop an alphabetic written language, that is, communicating with written words rather than pictures, until about 2000 BC. The book of Genesis was likely written by Moses about 1500 BC. So God's written revelation to humans actually began to be put into writing not that long after it was possible to do so. The reason God did not give Adam and Eve a written language is not given to us, although it may be somehow related to question 2.

Why doesn't God just reveal Himself to all humans in a way that "proves" His existence to everyone? He could communicate perfectly all He wants humans to know to each individual, making this whole discussion about "What is truth?" moot.

The answer to why He doesn't lies in the underlying message of the Bible: The most important characteristic God values in us humans is faith in Himself. Faith is belief in and trust of something that cannot be immediately verified by our senses. God has chosen to test our faith, each and every one of us, by not "proving" His existence in a way that is undeniable. He has chosen to give us a written revelation, a remarkably complete revelation, a revelation that has strong evidence of divine inspiration. Each of us needs to either accept or reject this revelation as truth.

Nothing in this chapter proves that the Christian Bible, the Old and New Testaments, is the Word of God. That is something that cannot be proved. Of course, neither can it be proved that Shakespeare wrote Romeo and Juliet, or that Thomas Jefferson wrote the Declaration of Independence, or that this book is made of atoms. We have strong evidence for all these claims. The difference is, what you believe about the authorship of Romeo and Juliet or the Declaration of Independence is of no great consequence. What you believe about God's involvement in the writing of the Bible, and its claims and promises, is an eternal life or death determining decision.

Oh yes, what did happen to all those men who contributed to the books of the Bible? What was their motive? Fame, fortune, power?

The Apostle Paul, who contributed much to the New Testament, was executed in Rome after being repeatedly arrested, jailed, and whipped for his teaching. The Apostle Matthew was murdered in Ethiopia after challenging the morality of King Hertacus. Luke, the physician, was martyred for his faith sometime around 84 AD. Simon Peter was crucified, upside down by some accounts, for preaching in Rome.

The Old Testament writers didn't fare much better. Moses lived a life hounded by the Israelites who never failed to complain bitterly when things got tough. He died prior to entering the promised land of Canaan. The prophets were often tasked to bring news of God's displeasure to the Israelites. Because of this, their lives were in constant danger. Although some are said to have died peacefully, others were brutally murdered. Isaiah was sawn in two by the Jewish King Manasseh. The prophet Jeremiah was stoned to death by Jews in Egypt. The prophet Ezekiel was murdered by the Chief of the Jews for rebuking his idolatry. David and Solomon were already wealthy kings prior to writing their contributions. It is not likely they gained anything for their efforts.

The Bible was written at great cost to many men. No one can reasonably claim that those who wrote it did so for personal gain. On the contrary, many lives were lost and many people suffered because of its content. Just one more evidence of its claim to be Truth.

4

A Tale of Two Testaments

Marcionism. The teaching that the God of the Old Testament and the God of the New Testament are different Gods, representing two different religions. Declared a heresy by the First Council of Nicea in 325.

Most Christians accept that both the Old and New Testaments belong in the written revelation of God to humans, the Bible. They are familiar with the stories of creation, the great flood and Noah's ark, Abraham's offering of his son as a sacrifice, the Israelites exodus from Egypt, and the killing of Goliath by David. Many can also recall the story of Ruth, the miraculous journey of Jonah, and some of the more famous psalms and proverbs. The familiar Old Testament stories are a staple for Sunday lessons during children's elementary school years.

What is less often read, either during Sunday worship, or in any Sunday school class, are the more gruesome and violent sections of text. God plays a prominent role in many of these accounts. In Exodus 12, God kills all the firstborn children in Egypt as one of the plagues delivered to Pharaoh for his continued defiance. Likely, thousands of people, including young children, died that night for Pharaoh's actions.

In Exodus 32, in response to the Israelites making and worshipping a golden calf, Moses says to the sons of Levi,

A TALE OF TWO TESTAMENTS

"Thus says the Lord, the God of Israel, 'Every man of you put his sword upon his thigh, and go back and forth from gate to gate in the camp, and kill every man his brother, and every man his friend, and every man his neighbor.'"

This slaughter among family and friends resulted in about 3000 deaths.

In Numbers 25 it is recorded for us that after a period when the Israelites bowed down to Baal and sacrificed to the Gods of the Moabites, *"The Lord said to Moses, 'Take all the leaders of the people and execute them in broad daylight before the Lord, so that the fierce anger of the Lord may turn away from Israel.'"* Moses then instructs the judges of Israel to slay all *"who have joined themselves to Baal of Peor."* Twenty-four thousand lose their life.

In another grisly account, after Elisha takes over the role of prophet from Elijah, he encounters a group of boys who mock his bald head. He curses them in the name of the Lord and a bear emerges from the woods and mauls 42 of them to death (2Ki 2:23,24).

What are we to make of all this killing and divine retribution? Doesn't it seem that these judgements are over the top, difficult to explain, or even believe? Aren't we taught in the New Testament that God is love? Isn't God supposed to be merciful and compassionate? Why is God described as angry (Num 22:22, 1 Ki 11:9, Ps 80:4) and jealous (Ex 20:5, Deut 4:24, Josh 24:19) in the Old Testament?

One thing is clear: the overall tenor of the 2 Testaments is clearly different. The Old Testament is full of uncensored, historical accounts of human interactions, highlighting the rebellious nature of man, and God's, often severe, reactions.

Intermingled throughout the whole of it is an abundance of God's law and His prophet's warnings of dire consequences for those who stray.

The New Testament begins with the appearance of Jesus of Nazareth, the ultimate game changer. Jesus comes teaching the arrival of the "Kingdom of God" (Mar 1:15) and a "New Covenant" (Heb 9:15). He talks about God's great love for the world (John 3:16) and summarizes God's law by saying, *"You shall love the Lord your God with all your heart, and with all your soul, and with all your strength, and with all your mind, and your neighbor as yourself"* (Luk 10:27). He challenges the Old Testament's prescription for justice: *"You have heard it said an eye for an eye and a tooth for a tooth. But I say to you do not resist an evil person; but whoever slaps you on the right cheek, turn the other to him also"* (Mat 5:38,39). He reframes the all-important Jewish Sabbath laws: *"The Sabbath was made for man, not man for the Sabbath"* (Mat 12:8), and demonstrates that He is Lord of the Sabbath by doing what was then considered unlawful on that holy day - healing and gathering food (Mt 12).

Jesus seemed to change everything. The overall doom and gloom of the Old Testament was changed to joy and thanksgiving in the New. The mass executions of the Old Testament were replaced by mass conversions to disciples of Christ. Rather than dogged adherence to laws about food and sacrifices and cleanliness, the New Testament teaches that we are free from the burden of obedience to these laws.

But why? Why did God, who says that He does not change (Mal 3:6), present such a different perspective of Himself in the Old Testament, only to have His Son change that perspective when He came to earth?

A TALE OF TWO TESTAMENTS

Suppose I walked up to a stranger and said to him emphatically, "You'd better get a lawyer to deal with your debt problem!" How do you think that person would react? Assuming he had no debt problem, he would likely think, "What a nutcase. Don't know what he is talking about. He's probably a lawyer looking for work." It would be very unlikely he would engage with me to find out why I thought he had such a pressing problem.

Humans have a huge debt problem. Most do not know it. Worse, most do not have any idea the consequences that await them for not dealing with this problem. God created humans as autonomous beings, morally responsible for their actions. Lions are not morally responsible for their actions. Neither are cockroaches, eagles, or chimpanzees. Humans are. God, in His abundant love, desired to rescue humans from their very large debt and impending destruction. His strategy to accomplish this was to first demonstrate to them how far, and often, they had strayed into debt, that is, sin. The rules, the law, needed to be clearly spelled out. This was done in detail and was delivered first to Moses, then to the Children of Israel, then to the rest of the world. Without knowing the law, people cannot know they have a debt problem.

The second step was to demonstrate the penalty for that sin. Talk is cheap. Threats of punishment have only a temporary restraining effect, especially if people don't ever see bad things happen. God's response to sin in the Old Testament, often thought severe or especially harsh, was actually quite restrained. The Divinely ascribed penalty for sin, *any sin*, is death (Rom 6:23). We humans like to make judgements about how bad a sin is. Murdering someone in cold blood or raping a young women is particularly heinous, and maybe, should be punished by death; but lying about my income to the IRS or having a little sex for fun during college is really pretty trivial, maybe even OK. These sins, if we are to even call them that, are certainly not worth an execution.

God's character requires perfect adherence to the law. Every person living during the time of the Old Testament deserved death. Everyone. Fortunately, in His mercy, He chose to display the true penalty for sin in relatively few people. God did not allow or direct slayings of persons who stole a handful of wheat from their neighbors field.

People were abruptly struck down for committing only certain sins, usually public sin involving the mocking of God or God's law. These were real world demonstrations of the penalty for sin. They served as a huge lesson to the people of that day, and were recorded to serve as a huge lesson for all who came after. The Old Testament is God's object lesson to the world, given to motivate them to seek a remedy.

It is only after people understand they have a very large debt and that the penalty for this debt is their very life, that people will urgently seek a remedy. Jesus of Nazareth was (and is) the remedy. Fully God and fully man, one with God the Father, He lived a perfect life and became the required sacrifice to pay for our sin.

The New Testament gives us the details of this remedy. In doing so, it also spells out what is expected of us in terms of mercy and compassion. In light of God's great provision for us, we, who are disciples of Christ, need to reflect that mercy and compassion to others. In this way, God's light can shine in and through us, and His image, incorporated into our being, can be demonstrated to all. Yes, we too all deserve death for our sin, just as those in Old Testament days, but the remedy has come and God's message to humanity has pivoted to highlight His great provision for our great debt.

But, here lies the danger. The church, especially the North American church, has progressively become more focused on the presentation of the remedy (The New Testament) to the exclusion of teaching our spiritual ancestor's experience before the arrival of Christ (the Old Testament). The Old Testament is messy. It's often unpleasant. It can be depressing. The degree to which the church is losing its grasp on the Old Testament is well documented in such recent books as The Old Testament is Dying (Brent Strawn, Baker Academic, 2017). Yet, we forget that when Jesus and the apostles spoke about "the Scriptures" in the New Testament, they were talking about the writings in the Old Testament. When Jesus said to the Sadducees, *"Is this not the reason you are mistaken, that you do not understand the Scriptures or the power of God?"* (Mar 12:24), He was pointing out their lack of knowledge of the Old Testament.

This decline in the Church's familiarity with the law and the prophets can easily lead to distortions in the Gospel. If God is mercy and compassion (and only mercy and compassion), then how can he sentence some people to eternal destruction?

I saw a truck driving around the other day in Chattanooga with a sticker on it that read, "Good news: we are all going to heaven." I would bet this person self-identifies as a Christian.

If God is love (and only love), then I expect He would love to bless me with health and prosperity all my days on this earth. People love to hear such things. Just take a look at how many people cram themselves into immense auditoriums to bask in the words of adoration and promises of blessings directed at themselves from certain teachers of the Gospel. God does bring blessings to His faithful followers, but by failing to convey God's abhorrence of sin, and His promises of judgement on those who live in sin, we can spread false and potentially eternally damaging teaching to people.

I was working in my clinic the other day and a woman was telling me her story of woes. She was telling me of her depression and anxiety and her struggles making it day to day. When I asked her about the relationships in her life, she told me a rather long tale of the various men she had lived with and the fights they had over their drug use. The current man she was with was getting her involved in stealing to support his substance abuse, resulting in her current high level of anxiety. When I asked if she had any connection to a church she said, "Well, I don't go to church but I am a Christian which is a good thing since I am forgiven for anything bad I do."

Apparently this woman had learned that that is what Christianity was all about - signing up for a get-out-of-jail-free card; that her activities and actions in this life have no bearing on how God will judge her.

Churches that teach only about God's love and grace while downplaying or ignoring God's justice and judgement are teaching only half the truth. God has many characteristics, and these all need to be taught to insure we are not painting a picture of God as the divine vending machine, meeting all our earthly desires with the push of a button. Studying the Old Testament helps to reinforce all the attributes of God, not just those that make us feel warm and cuddly.

It is true that the Old Testament contains the Old Covenant - or more precisely the Old Covenants. The New Testament contains the New Covenant brought by Christ to a world in need. The New Covenant supersedes the Old Covenants since it represents God's final provision and promise regarding the path to salvation. The New Covenant is expressed most succinctly in John 3:16: *"For God so loved the world that He gave His only Son, that whoever believes in Him may not perish but have eternal life."* The Old Covenants, discussed in more detail in chapter 5, were necessary and instructive for God's people as they awaited the arrival of the Messiah. The fact that they have been replaced does not mean that they should be thrown into the dustbin of useless information. Just as spending time in a history museum can reveal much about who we are and how we arrived at our present situation, so too spending time in the Old Testament can bring a fuller understanding of God's weaving together human history to bring about the salvation of His children.

I had said earlier in this chapter that the arrival of Jesus seemed to change everything. What about the law? What effect did Jesus' life, death, and resurrection have on His followers' duty to obey the law?

This question has challenged the Church since its inception. Does Old Testament law still apply to New Testament people? Didn't Jesus come to take the law off our backs? Should Christians all be eating Kosher and should they be circumcising their boys? What about all the sacrifices? What about all the Sabbath laws?

Most laws given to us in the Old Testament can be placed into one of three general categories. First are the laws given to govern the behaviors of people one to another. Second are the laws regarding our relationship with God. Third, are the prophetic laws, that is, laws concerning actions that pointed to the coming of the Messiah. The first two groups of laws were almost exclusively given in the form of "You shall not," while the latter group in the form of "You shall." In other words, laws about how we are to relate to one another and God were given in terms of unacceptable behaviors (e.g. lying, stealing), while the laws given to foreshadow the New Covenant were given in terms of prescribed behaviors (e.g. sin offerings, peace offerings). Realizing that the Old Testament laws can be categorized in this fashion helps immensely when trying to decide how we should regard them today.

Starting with the latter category, laws that point to Christ, it makes sense that once Christ was revealed, these laws would become obsolete. For over a thousand years, the nation of Israel served as the world's herald, announcing through their actions and through their prophets what God's requirements were for redemption. Christ would come and shed His blood on our behalf to satisfy the judgement of God. Until that event occurred, however, the blood of animals would be shed to provide a vivid reminder of the awful truth: *"without shedding of blood there is no forgiveness"* (Heb 9:22).

The temple of the Lord was a bloody place in those days. Blood was wiped on the altar, poured around its base and sprinkled on the floor (Lev 3:2-13). The priests offered sacrifices in this manner every day. Although there is no point blank directive in the New Testament which states, "Stop the sacrifices," the writer of Hebrews indicates these sacrifices are no longer needed. In naming Jesus as our perfect High Priest he says,

> *"For it was fitting for us to have such a high priest, holy, innocent, undefiled, separated from sinners and exalted above the heavens; who does not need daily, like those high priests, to offer up sacrifices, first for His own sins and then for the sins of the people, because this He did once for all when He offered up Himself"* (Heb 7:26,27).

Jesus was the point of all the sacrifices the children of Israel were commanded to present to God. The final sacrifice has been offered - no further sacrifices are needed or are appropriate. Interestingly, about 40 years after the crucifixion of Jesus, even the priests of Israel who rejected Jesus as Messiah stopped offering sacrifices. When the temple was destroyed in 70 AD, the sacrifices halted, but curiously, never resumed, at least not in any organized or consistent fashion. The leaders of Israel could have erected a temporary temple or tabernacle to continue their centuries long obedience to the sacrificial laws, but they did not. To this day, the Jewish nation offers no sacrifices despite no prophecy or revelation retracting the commands to do so. Perhaps God has demonstrated the sufficiency of Jesus' sacrifice even through those who have rejected Him.

As for the other two categories of laws, both are represented and summarized in the 10 commandments. First appearing in Scripture in Exodus 20, and repeated in Deuteronomy 5, the first 4 give commands about how we are to relate to God and the last 6 how we are to relate to each other. We are to worship only one God, who is not to be represented by any idol, and whose name is to be held in honor. We are to remember the Sabbath day to keep it holy. We are to not murder, steal, lie, or commit adultery. We are to honor our parents and to not covet anything that is our neighbors. Nine of these commandments are plainly restated in the New Testament giving us no doubt that they apply to us today. (Mat 4:10, Acts 17:29, 1 Tim 6:1, Eph 6:1, Rom 13:9)

The New Testament treatment of the fourth commandment, *"Remember the Sabbath day to keep it holy"* (Ex 20:8), is a bit more complex. The word "Sabbath" occurs in 55 verses in the New Testament - too many to go through verse by verse here. About half of those verses contain incidental mentions about something occurring on the Sabbath. Most of the other verses are situations where Jesus is either being accused of breaking Sabbath law or Jesus is challenging the Pharisees about what is, or is not, lawful on the Sabbath. Looking back at Exodus 20, the fourth commandment is followed by some instructions about how we are to remember the Sabbath:

Six days you shall labor and do all your work, but the seventh day is a Sabbath to the Lord your God; in it you shall not do any work, you or your son, or your daughter, or your male or your female servant or your cattle or your sojourner who stays with you (vv 9,10).

In the centuries after that command was given, the leaders of Israel added their own instructions about what would be prohibited on the Sabbath. They defined "work" for the people in very specific terms, ostensibly so that everyone would be very clear about what could lawfully be done on a Sabbath day and what could not. Included in "work" was planting, grinding wheat, baking bread, weaving 2 threads together, tying knots, killing animals, building, making a fire, putting out a fire, and writing 2 or more letters.[1] When Jesus and his disciples picked some wheat on the Sabbath, the Pharisees were quick to point out that this broke one of their Sabbath restrictions (Mat 12:1,2). When Jesus chose to heal on the Sabbath, this too was deemed work by the Pharisees, and thus a breaking of Sabbath law (Mar 3:1-6). Jesus responds to both criticisms by pointing out that the Sabbath was meant to bless us, not to make life hard for us (Mar 2:27).

There is no place in the New Testament where we are instructed to stop remembering the Sabbath day. Jesus observed the Sabbath "as was His custom" (Luk 4:16). We *are* instructed to stop judging one another about how we individually celebrate the Sabbath. Paul says to the Colossians, *"Therefore no one is to act as your judge in regard to food or drink or in respect to a festival or a new moon or a Sabbath day"* (2:16).

We, in keeping with Jesus' example, are to "remember the Sabbath day to **keep it holy**," by setting aside time to worship, pray, rest from our labors, and glory in the goodness of our God. In our present time, a time when the Sabbath is largely ignored, we should be encouraging one another to remember that God is our rest, our rescuer from this fallen world, and provider of our redemption that comes through faith in Christ.

Jesus summarized all 10 commandments for His followers in the positive (rather than the negative - "you shall not") by saying,

> *"You shall love the Lord your God with all your heart, and with all your soul, and with all your strength, and with all your mind; and your neighbor as yourself"* (Luk 10:27).

He did not stop there, however. Just in case anyone thought he, or she, was keeping this "law of love" perfectly, He clarified what was really required to be a keeper of the 10 commandments. In Matthew 5, Jesus says to His followers,

> *"You have heard that the ancients were told, 'You shall not commit murder,' and 'Whoever commits murder shall be liable to the courts.' But I say to you that everyone who is angry with his brother shall be guilty before the court; and whoever says to his brother, 'You good-for-nothing,' shall be guilty before the supreme court; and whoever says, 'You fool,' shall be guilty enough to go into the fiery hell"* (Mat 5:21,22).

Jesus continues by pointing out men's sexual sin:

> *"You have heard that it was said, 'You shall not commit adultery;' but I say to you that everyone who looks at a woman with lust for her has already committed adultery with her in his heart"* (vv 27,28).

With that pronouncement, Jesus just convicted all men of adultery. There would be no self-congratulation about perfect obedience to the letter of the law. In just these few verses, Jesus declares that all people are law breakers. He also affirms that such lawbreaking is worthy of being sent to hell!

Later in this same chapter, Jesus makes some additional surprising statements. Starting in verse 38 Jesus says, *"You have heard that it was said, 'An eye for an eye and a tooth for a tooth.' But I say to you, do not resist an evil person; but whoever slaps you on the right cheek, turn to him the other also."*

This was certainly something the Jews had never heard anyone say before. Was Jesus changing the law here in regards to how we are to treat one another? Not really. He didn't say, "Slapping your neighbor across the face is now OK." Assault was against the law in the Old Testament, and is still a sin in the New Testament era. What Jesus was saying was that our response to sin should reflect God's mercy shown to us. An eye for an eye is pure justice, as is a life for a life. The Old Testament laws were given along with corresponding punishments for breaking these laws. Those punishments reflected pure justice as defined by God, although as noted above, breaking any of the laws, from God's perspective, makes us guilty of them all (James 2:10). Rather than respond to sin in a manner that reflects pure justice, we are now to consider mercy in our response. The definition of right and wrong has not changed.

A couple of other aspects of Old Testament law need to be mentioned before closing. In Leviticus 11 and Deuteronomy 14, dietary laws are given to Moses. These chapters provide a list of food the children of Israel were not to eat (unclean food) along with a complementary list of food that was acceptable (clean food). The designations "clean" and "unclean" are key to understanding what this was all about. If, by these designations, God was protecting the Israelites from an intrinsic danger in the food, such as increased infection risk or other risk to their health, then this wouldn't change with the coming of Christ. If, however, the designation held one of spiritual significance, such as a reminder that only God can make things "clean", then these laws would more naturally fall into the category of prophetic laws. The expectation would then be that with the advent of Christ, the observance of these dietary restrictions would cease.

Reading through the New Testament, we find no mention of any dietary restrictions. On the contrary, Jesus and the apostles specifically address the issue of "unclean" food in numerous passages. In Mark 7, Jesus is once again being accused of breaking Old Testament law by not performing the ritual washing before eating, which had been instituted by the Israeli leaders. Jesus shows his irritation with their overt legalism by stating,

> *"Rightly did Isaiah prophesy of you hypocrites, as it is written: 'This people honors me with their lips, but their heart is far from me. But in vain do they worship me, teaching as doctrines the precepts of men.' Neglecting the commandment of God, you hold to the tradition of men" (vv 6,7).*

He then proceeds to call them out over their traditions in caring for their elderly parents that led to personal benefit at the expense of their parent's wellbeing (vv 10-13), thus breaking the fifth commandment. Lastly, He says this to His followers,

> *"Listen to Me, all of you, and understand: there is nothing outside the man which can defile him if it goes into him; but the things which proceed out of the man are what defile the man" (vv 14,15).*

Wait! Did Jesus just negate all the dietary laws in one sentence? Over 14 centuries of carefully picking and preparing food so as not to be contaminated by something "unclean," suddenly made no longer necessary? This would be a dramatic change for all Jews. His disciples, understandably, wanted some confirmation. Jesus expands on His statement for His disciple's sake in verses 17 through 19:

> *When He had left the crowd and entered the house, His disciples questioned Him about the parable. And He said to them, "Are you so lacking in understanding also? Do you not understand that whatever goes into the man from outside cannot defile him, because it does not go into his heart, but into his stomach, and is eliminated?" (Thus He declared all foods clean.)*

Yes, Jesus was relieving all Jews from the burden of following the dietary laws. The parenthetical statement "Thus He declared all foods clean" was written by the apostle Mark, under the inspiration of the Holy Spirit, to make it clear to all that this was in fact what Jesus was saying. It was such a big change, he likely felt compelled to spell it out so very clearly since he knew that many would fail to be convinced otherwise.

Scripture tells us that even some apostles were not immediately convinced. In the book of Acts, a few months after Jesus resurrection, Peter is being prepared to meet and witness to a Gentile, someone considered "unclean." The Spirit brings a vision to Peter 3 times:

> *And he [Peter] saw the sky opened up, and an object like a great sheet coming down, lowered by four corners to the ground, and there were in it all kinds of four-footed animals and crawling creatures of the earth and birds of the air. A voice came to him, "Get up, Peter, kill and eat!" But Peter said, "By no means, Lord, for I have*

never eaten anything unholy or unclean." Again a voice came to him a second time, "What God has cleansed, no longer consider unholy" (Acts 10:11-14).

Peter correctly makes the connection that God is removing the "unclean" designation from not only food, but people also, specifically the Gentiles (v 28). They too, can be recipients of the Holy Spirit. (v 45) Gentile believers were to be baptized and welcomed into the body of Christ (vv 47,48). Peter's vision supports the classification of the dietary laws in the prophetic category; laws meant to point to the coming of the Messiah and the New Covenant. There are some church leaders today who claim that Peter's vision was *only* about the acceptance of Gentiles and had nothing to do with food. That certain foods should still be considered unclean, just not people. If this were so, it would be highly confusing, especially since the Spirit caused the vision to be recorded for us so carefully in Scripture. Why use the unclean food to show Peter the new reality, and why have God command Peter, "Kill and eat?" It would make no sense. It would also contradict the clear statement given to us in the Gospel of Mark.

The apostle Paul concurs that food restrictions no longer apply to New Testament believers. In both 1 Corinthians chapter 8 and chapter 10, Paul goes to great lengths to explain that food sacrificed to idols is no longer to be considered defiled and thus off limits for eating. He does strongly urge believers to consider the impact on others of such eating and to not injure the conscience of another. But, the Old Testament prohibition against such eating is no longer in effect. Also, as quoted above in Colossians 2:16, he expressly includes one's food and drink as something that should be above criticism. There is full agreement throughout the New Testament that no food should now be considered "unclean."

Finally, a look at the laws regarding sexual sin. These laws involve our relationship one to another. The Old Testament clearly, and sometimes graphically, presents its prohibition against adultery, fornication, incest, homosexuality, and bestiality. These laws are presented in the form, "You shall not." They are represented by the 7th commandment, "You shall not commit adultery," and thus they form a group with the commands against murder, lying, and stealing. Yet, in our present day, especially in the United States and Europe, fornication and homosexuality are considered at least morally neutral, if not fully acceptable behaviors. Those who speak out against such behavior are labeled bigots or religious zealots or homophobes.

Is there any reason to think that the coming of Jesus changed God's mind about these behaviors? We saw previously that Jesus singled out adultery as a sin in Matthew 5. Later, in Matthew 19, He recites the laws that are needed for righteousness, "You shall not murder; you shall not commit adultery; you shall not steal; you shall not bear false witness" (v18). Adultery continues to be on the list of God's forbidden behaviors. Fornication also is specifically identified as sin in the New Testament:

> *Gal 5:19,20 Now the works of the flesh are evident, which are: adultery, fornication, uncleanness, lewdness, idolatry, sorcery, hatred, contentions, jealousies, outbursts of wrath, selfish ambitions, dissensions, heresies. (NKJ)*

> *Eph 5:3 But fornication and all uncleanness or covetousness, let it not even be named among you, as is fitting for saints. (NKJ)*

> *Heb 13:4 Marriage is to be held in honor among all,*

and the marriage bed is to be undefiled; for fornicators and adulterers God will Judge.

Homosexuality and same sex marriage have been particularly contentious issues over the past 20 years, but since the striking down of laws against these once taboo practices in the US and elsewhere, they have gained acceptance, even in the church. In Old Testament times, homosexuality was considered a particularly heinous offense, along with adultery and bestiality, all three carrying the punishment of death. Leviticus 20:13 makes this crystal clear: "If there is a man who lies with a male as those who lie with a woman, both of them have committed a detestable act; they shall surely be put to death." And Leviticus 18:22: "You shall not lie with a male as one lies with a female; it is an abomination."

The New Testament is not silent regarding homosexuality. Homosexuality is called "unholy and profane" by Timothy:

But we know that the law is good, if one uses it lawfully, realizing the fact that the law is not made for a righteous person, but for those who are lawless and rebellious, for the ungodly and sinners, for the unholy and profane, for those who kill their fathers and mothers, for murderers and immoral men and homosexuals, and kidnappers and liars and perjurers, and whatever else is contrary to sound teaching (1 Ti 1:8-10).

The Apostle Paul tells the Corinthians,

"Or do you not know that the unrighteous will not inherit the kingdom of God? Do not be deceived; neither fornicators, nor idolaters, nor adulterers, nor effeminate, nor homosexuals, nor thieves, nor the covetous, nor drunkards, nor revilers, nor swindlers, will inherit the kingdom of God" (1 Co 6:9,10).

Homosexuality continues to be seriously offensive to God. It is disqualifying for entry into His heavenly kingdom. The church is guilty of doing great damage to people if it pretends, or teaches, that God is OK with sexual activity between two men or two women.

In summary, the Old and New Testaments form a complete and complementary revelation of God. They should both be diligently studied in order to maintain a balanced view of God's mercy and compassion alongside his justice and judgement. Although the Old Testament highlights God's law, and humanity's dismal failures in obedience to that law, God's love and mercy are also presented, most profoundly in His prophesies of a rescuer for His people (Gen 3:15, Is 53). The New Testament opens with the arrival of this great rescuer, the Messiah, the Christ, who lives a perfect life and sheds His blood for our sin. The New Testament closes with images of God's final judgement, a great and terrible day, when those who believe and trust in Jesus as Lord will inherit eternal life, and those who do not will be sentenced to eternal destruction.

A TALE OF TWO TESTAMENTS

5

In the Beginning

On June 22, 1633, a man named Galileo Galilei was found guilty of heresy by the Catholic Church. What teaching prompted his trial and sentence? For years Galileo had taught that the earth was not stationary, but rather revolved on its axis and orbited around the sun. The church's official teaching up to that point was that the earth was the center of the universe and all planetary bodies, including the sun, revolved around the earth. His sentence was house arrest for the rest of his life.

Though this sounds a bit crazy to us now, there were many good reasons for the church to teach "geocentrism." First of all, it doesn't feel like the earth is moving. We know now that the surface of the earth is moving at about 1000 miles per hour, but since our atmosphere is moving at roughly the same speed, we don't experience any sense of this movement. The church was not interested in propagating interesting theories that went against people's everyday experience.

Second, the language that was used at that time, and is still used, to describe the sun's "movement" makes it sound like we are still, while the sun arcs overhead. The sun "rises" in the east and "sets" in the west. The sun "goes down." The sun "makes it way across the sky." No one says, "We've rotated past the point where the sun becomes visible above the horizon," to report a sunrise.

Third, and most importantly for the church, there are numerous biblical texts that use language that seem to indicate the earth is still and everything above our heads is rotating around us. 1 Chronicles 16:30 says, "Tremble before Him, all the earth; Indeed the world is firmly established, it will not be moved." Ecclesiastes 1:5 reads, "Also, the sun rises and the sun sets; And hastening to its place it rises there again." And of course, Joshua 10:13: "So the sun stood still and the moon stopped, until the nation avenged themselves of their enemies. Is it not written in the book of Jashar? And the sun stopped in the middle of the sky and did not hasten to go down for about a whole day." Such verses led church leaders to defend their strong belief in a stationary earth.

Except for a few isolated exceptions[1], the worldwide Christian church long ago abandoned geocentrism in favor of heliocentrism - the understanding that the sun is the center of our solar system. What caused the church to change its position? Why were interpretations of the above verses altered?

Abundant, consistent, and compelling observational evidence caused the change. This evidence, what the church calls Natural Revelation, consists of everything our senses take in on a daily basis. God created the universe, and it is reasonable that we can learn much about God by studying what He has made. In this instance, Natural Revelation helped us come to a clearer and more accurate understanding of how to interpret many biblical passages.

In the quest to understand how our world came to be, its creation, along with the creation of every living being, we should take into consideration God's communication to us through the Canon **and** through Natural Revelation. The Bible itself states,

"The heavens declare His righteousness and all the peoples have seen His glory" (Ps 97:6), and *"For since the creation of the world His invisible attributes, His eternal power and divine nature, have been clearly seen, being understood through what has been made, so that they are without excuse"* (Rom 1:20).

We were meant to use our 5 senses and our reason to experience the goodness of God, to worship God, and to gain an understanding of God's supreme power and intellect. The technological advances and growth of knowledge that have occurred over the last 100 years have only deepened our wonder at the size, design, and complexity of everything that exists. Even the simplest living organisms display unbelievably fine-tuned chemical reactions that allow them to reproduce, to use energy to do work, and to battle outside forces that threaten their survival. All life is "fearfully and wonderfully made" (Ps 139:14).

Genesis 1 is by far the most scrutinized text when it comes to describing the creation of the universe and life on planet earth, but Genesis 2 also contains information that must not be ignored. Both must be considered to gain a complete picture of what happened "In the beginning." Both must also be squared with what God shows us in our exploration of what He has created.

But what if what we see and touch contradicts what is said in Genesis? Shouldn't we decide to ignore what we see in favor of what we read? Or shouldn't we say to ourselves, "What I'm seeing must be an illusion or must have been purposefully altered by God. What the Bible says takes precedence over anything my senses or reason tells me."

Although it is certainly true that our senses and reason sometimes fail us, it is not true that God designed our senses or reason to lead us to wrong conclusions. When they do, it is due to malfunction or faulty logic, neither of which are characteristics of our Creator. Any apparent conflict between Scripture and what we can plainly see and measure must be resolved in a rational way - to leave it unresolved or to encourage resolution by dismissing the Scripture as "myth" or our human experience as "deluded" declares that God has intentionally deceived us. This proposition is incompatible with the biblical description of God as "Truth."

The Creation

The written revelation of God to humans begins, *"In the beginning God created ..."* (Gen 1:1). These 5 words set the stage for all of history. Our history began with the creative action of God.

It is always a bit shocking to me when I hear anyone, especially those working in science-related fields, say they do not believe in the existence of God, and that everything we see is the result of the random association of atoms. This is irrational. It is in no way supported by science.

Every day in this country, thousands of labs mix together the building blocks of life: hydrogen, oxygen, carbon, nitrogen. These mixtures are subjected to heat and cold, radiation and electromagnetic fields. Not once has a living cell emerged from such a mixture. Not once. Even when we put the exact right amounts of these elements together and carefully add energy in ways that are conducive to chemical reactions - nothing. So, the spontaneous emergence of life from non-life is completely unsupported by experimental science. In fact, what 100 years of intense scientific experimentation has taught us is that life does not create itself.

Thinking that complex biological life could arise by random chance is more irrational than claiming that a functioning iPhone 8 could somehow form itself into existence in a bubbling Yellowstone mud pot, complete with touchscreen, lithium ion battery, integrated circuit chips, GPS capability, and the bitten apple logo in just the right place. No person would ever make such a claim because it is clearly absurd. Yet there are those who have been trained in the sciences, willing to make that basic claim about the human body. That's irrational.

God, a being of unfathomable intelligence and power, created life. Genesis 1:1 tells us He (using the pronoun given to us in Scripture) started by creating matter (v 1). At some point later, he created energy in the form of light (v 3). After the creation of energy, Scripture uses a phrase that is repeated 5 times in the rest of the chapter: *"And there was evening and there was morning, one day."*

The meaning of the word "day" (Heb, yom) used in these verses has been highly contested. Given the use of the words "evening" and "morning" right before it, a natural interpretation would be that this means a 24-hour period of time. It certainly could be. God could have created light in the first 24-hour period of time, and then followed this by creating everything else mentioned in Genesis 1 during 5 other consecutive 24-hour periods of time. But before assigning this as the "right" meaning, we need to consider other plausible possibilities.

The Hebrew word "yom," which is used many times in the Old Testament, does not always mean 24 hours. In fact, "yom" more generally refers to "a period of time." We can see this right off the bat in verse 5 of Genesis:

> *God called the light day* (yom*), and the darkness He called night. And there was evening and there was*

morning, one day (yom).

So, in this single verse, "yom" is used 2 different ways - to indicate the time of light (~ 12 hours in the earth-day scenario) and to indicate a full day/night cycle, or 24 hours. In other Old Testament verses, "yom" is used for "time" (Gen 4:3), "year" (Amos 4:4), "season" (Joshua 24:7), and "age" (multiple - Gen 18 and 24, Josh 23). Any of these meanings, then, are possible. Still, the "evening" and "morning" language in these verses might cause us to lean toward a strict 24-hour interpretation.

Are there any reasons that a 24-hour period of time may not be the best meaning for "day" in Genesis 1?

It turns out there are many. First, we define a "day" by the time it takes the earth to rotate once around its axis. Because of the presence of our sun and moon, we can say that each day includes one morning and one evening. If we look closely at Genesis 1, we note that during the first 3 "days" of creation, our sun and moon didn't exist. With no sun, there would be no way to mark one rotation of the earth, if the earth was even rotating. With no sun, there would be no sun setting (evening) and no sun rising (morning).

These words (morning, evening) cannot, then, have the same meaning we give to them, at least in the first 13 verses of Genesis. Alternate meanings are reasonable. They could mean: "evening" - the period of time when one's work is finished, and "morning" - the period of time when work is to begin again. This meaning would certainly be one that is consistent with all the verses that deal with God's creative work.

A second problem with the strict 24-hour meaning for "day" is that this restricts God's creative activities to time periods that don't make much rational sense. God could have created everything we see in 10 nanoseconds. Why would He stretch that period to 144 hours (6 earth days)?

During "day" 1, God created energy by saying, *"let there be light."* How long do we suppose this took? Probably instantaneous. It is unclear why He would then wait 23 plus hours to start work on expanding the universe to its present size.

On "day" 2 God creates the space for the universe by separating a massive ball of water (likely the first molecule made) into a smaller, central ball and a spherical shell of water around it with space (a lot of space) in between. (If we ever get to the outer reaches of the universe, we shouldn't be surprised to find water there.) Again, this took however long God chose it to take, but thinking this was done in the time it takes the earth (which was then a ball of water) to rotate once on its axis in relation to the sun (which didn't exist yet) and that God timed this to conform to a future human understanding of what a "day" is, seems to straightjacket God into a schedule of our making.

On "day" 6, God creates all animal life, including humans. In Genesis 2 we read that before God made the first human female (Eve), He asked the first male (Adam) to name all the animals that had been created (Gen 2:19). It is not known, of course, how many species of animals there were at that time, but since the earth currently is home to over 8 million species of animals, of which over 5000 are mammals, having them all named during part of a day (presumably when there was light) does not seem reasonable.

Looking back at what happened on "day" 3, God forms the continents on earth and arranges the water into seas (1:9,10). He also creates all plant life. Note the wording:

Let the earth sprout vegetation, plants yielding seed, and fruit trees on the earth bearing fruit after their kind with seed in them (v 11). The earth brought forth vegetation, plants yielding seed after their kind, and trees bearing fruit with seeds in them after their kind (v 12).

So on "day" 3, after God created the dry land, plant life "sprouted", grew into mature plants and trees, and bore fruit, all in a matter of hours. Again, it just doesn't make sense to cram all of this into one earth day. Yes, God can do the miraculous, and could have forced all of His new biological creations to mature at rates far beyond their current capabilities, but why would He? I imagine that He quite enjoyed the creative process, just as we humans do, and wouldn't have a reason to forcibly rush this process to stick to some schedule determined by the earth's spin.

The third and most compelling reason to dismiss the 24-hour interpretation of "day" is God's Natural Revelation. If God created everything over 6 earth-days, and the genealogies contained in Scripture are not missing vast amounts of information, then the universe would be roughly 6000 years old (the position of "young earth creationists"). But the universe tells a very different story. Everywhere we look, whether it be toward the sun, or the stars, or at the earth, or the earth's record of history contained in geologic formations and biologic fossils, it all points to a universe much, much older. A universe knit together masterfully over billions of our earth years. Visual evidence that is consistent, robust, and that matches the order presented in Genesis 1.

Rather than go into the intricacies of radioactive isotope dating or silt analysis or spectral descriptions of incoming electromagnetic fields (all of which speak against a 6000 year old earth), a more familiar topic proves the point. Dinosaurs and humans did not live at the same time. How do we know? Three ways:

1. If humans and dinos lived at the same time, humans would have eaten dinosaurs and dinosaurs would have eaten humans. We have vast amounts of fossilized animal waste, both from humans and dinosaurs. Yet, there are no traces of human DNA in dino dung and no traces of dino DNA in human dung. This evidence should be relatively easy to find if it existed.

2. Dinos are extinct, humans are not. If Adam and dinos were created on the same day about 6000 years ago, then all the dinos went extinct within a couple thousand years. Whatever caused their extinction would also have wiped out humans if they were sharing the same real estate. (Noah was told to gather a pair of all the animals on earth, so this would have saved them from the flood, if they still existed).

3. If humans and dinos lived at the same time, humans would have killed and used dino parts for everything - bones for tools, skins for rugs and clothing, teeth and claws for jewelry, and tusks for decoration. And since we know that dinosaurs covered the earth in large numbers, these human uses of dino body parts would be seen in all cultures, in every household. But that is not what we see. There is no evidence that humans killed and used dinosaur parts as a routine part of their daily lives. That is because, dinosaurs and humans did not live at the same time.

Using the meaning "age" for the Hebrew "yom" in Genesis 1 resolves all the problems presented thus far. God created the universe, and life on this planet, over the course of 6 distinct "ages." The length of these ages is not given to us in Scripture, but observation of the universe gives us some idea of each of their lengths.[2] Abandoning the six 24-hour day understanding of creation does raise some questions about other biblical texts which will be addressed in the objections section of this chapter.

Evolution

What about evolution? Didn't humans evolve from lower life forms? Don't we have good scientific evidence in the fossil record that proves we humans came from a common primate ancestor?

The word "evolution" has become synonymous with "Darwinian evolution," the theory that life spontaneously formed itself, and over millions of years, gradually improved itself, resulting in what we see around us today. These improvements, so the evolutionists claim, occurred by random changes in the plant or animal's molecular structures. Random changes that were good changes stuck because those helped the organism survive and multiply, and changes that were bad quickly disappeared, along with the unfortunate organism that experienced those changes. On the surface it sounds like it could have happened. Certainly, most schools teach this as established fact, long ago dropping the word "theory."

The problem with this theory is that it is not possible. Darwinian evolution didn't happen.

The key to understanding why this is so is DNA - deoxyribonucleic acid. DNA is a visually gorgeous, spiral shaped molecule, that contains all the information required for the formation and maintenance of life. No living organism exists without DNA. Life is not possible without it.

In order to get a sense of what DNA is like, and how it works, picture 1 inch square blocks, each being one of four colors (red, green, blue, yellow), stacked on top of one another. The number of blocks needed to encode the information necessary for the simplest living organism, a bacterial cell, is about 3 million. That's a 48 mile high stack (The stack height for a human would be 48,000 miles). The sequence of colors - for example, red, blue, green, blue, yellow, red, yellow, etc - determines what that organism will look like and how it will function. The sequence is the blueprint. It cannot be changed without changing the organism.

Now, forget for a moment that life does not spontaneously create itself. Forget that it takes protein to make DNA and it takes DNA to make protein (Worth pondering for a while). Forget that all the parts of a cell (DNA, ribosomes, cell wall, mitochondria) would have to come together simultaneously for a cell to "come to life." Imagine that these facts aren't true and that a few million atoms arranged themselves together just right to produce the first living cell. Sometime later, this cell wants to improve itself by becoming a 2 celled organism. In order for this to happen, it needs to acquire at least 2 new proteins (it actually would need more than this, but for the sake of argument...). The first of these is an adhesion protein to bind the new 2 celled organism together, and the other a cell wall communication protein that would allow the 2 cells to share information. Each of these proteins will take about 1000 blocks of information to make.

According to Darwinian evolution, the cell will gain this new information through random mutations, or changes, in the cell's current DNA. One way these changes can occur is when the DNA is replicating; one color can be substituted for another. Unfortunately, this sort of change, a substitution in the sequence, will only get the cell killed by altering proteins it needs to survive. What the cell needs is new information, not changes to its existing information.

The cell needs 2000 new blocks in just the right sequence. The cell can't get these 2000 new blocks one at a time. If a single new block is inserted into the existing string, it changes the whole way the code is read (for the formation of proteins, blocks are read 3 at a time), and the cell dies. It is true that cells can steal sections of DNA from other cells, which can give them new proteins, but this is the first cell type, stealing sections from other cells will only replicate information it already has. The cell does not have the chemical machinery to string together random colored blocks of information to make a new string; that would kill the cell by strangling it with unending useless strings of blocks. The cell only has chemical machinery to replicate current DNA. It's not possible for the cell to get the information it needs to "evolve" to something bigger and better.

The only way for this single cell to gain the information it needs to become a 2 celled organism is the same way the cell phone went from being a clunky brick to a sleek, multifunctional computer: an intelligent being designed the necessary improvements and reconstructed the device putting the new parts in place all at once.

In the case of life, God, through a series of countless, mind boggling enhancements, generated millions of different types of organisms - all the diversity of life we currently see along with every type of animal and plant that no longer exists. Some call this explanation of how God went about creating life on earth "progressive creationism." This process is consistent with both the biblical record of creation as well as the record of history God has given us in our universe.

Genesis 1 gives us an overview of that entire creation process, while Genesis 2 gives us a more intimate look at God's creation of, and His relationship to, humans. When comparing the 2 chapters, there do seem to be some inconsistencies. Why might this be?

Imagine someone flying over the Grand Canyon in Arizona at 20,000 feet. This person is tasked to write a description of the whole canyon for those who have never seen it. A different person is given the same task, however this person is hiking down from the top to the bottom of the canyon. How might their descriptions differ?

It's likely they would differ in all sorts of ways. The hiker would describe the terrain, details about the plants and animals, and expressions of awesomeness at its height (once at the bottom). The pilot would describe the canyon's overall shape, colors, and depth. Very different descriptions of the same geological formation. Likewise, it's not surprising that the 2 perspectives in Genesis 1 and 2 don't match each other in all their details.

In regards to the creation of humans, Genesis 1 tells us that *"God created man in His image"* (v 27). This description is unique to humans. God did not create anything else *"in His image."* A curious phrase, but what might this mean?

This phrase cannot mean that we physically look like God. God is Spirit (Jn 4:24). God can adopt human form, or any form for that matter, but in essence, God is Spirit. Being made in the "image" of God must mean we share certain attributes of God that are not shared by other living organisms. Some of these attributes can be plainly seen: humans can communicate complex and abstract ideas using various languages; humans can design and create complicated machinery as well as sophisticated art; humans possess a sense of what constitutes right and appropriate behavior as well as what is wrong, reprehensible behavior; and humans are able to express feelings such as regret, joy, guilt, and admiration in ways unknown to other animals.

There are some other less obvious characteristics that God instilled only into humans. One is possession of a spirit. No other animal is said to have a spirit. Another is the ability to have a relationship with God that involves trust and worship.

Adam and Eve were the first 2 humans created. They were the pinnacle of God's creative work; beings that He could communicate with on a personal level. Beings with the intelligence to plan, create, evaluate, and pursue goals. With this intelligence also came the responsibility of making choices. Some of these choices were morally neutral (like what to name that fuzzy creature up in the tree), while others involved choosing obedience to God's instructions versus following a desire contrary to God's will.

We read in Genesis 2, God *"planted a garden toward the east, in Eden, and there He placed the man whom He had formed"* (v 8). Verse 15 tells us God *"put him [Adam] into the garden to cultivate it and keep it."* At this point, Adam could have looked around and said "No thanks, God. Gardening is not for me." There is no evidence that he did this. God also instructed Adam to name all the animals that He had created (v 19). Again, Adam complied. In verse 16, God gives Adam the command, *"From any tree in the garden you may eat freely; but from the tree of the knowledge of good and evil you shall not eat, for in the day that you eat from it, you shall surely die."*

You would think Adam's choice in this matter would be quite clear. Lots of trees and plants to eat from. One to avoid. Seriously bad consequences for me if the choice is made to disobey God's command. Yet, eventually, Adam does decide to follow his own desires despite God's clear instructions. This moral failure, this rebellion against the Creator of the universe, this statement that man's desires are more important than God's, sets in motion the great redemptive plan of our perfectly just, perfectly loving God.

Two important objections have been offered to this interpretation of Scripture regarding the timing and manner of God's creative work:

Objection 1: "The wages of sin is death." (Rom 6:23) If death is due to sin, then before Adam and Eve sinned, there must not have been any death. Thus, the earth could not be billions of years old since that would require billions of years of plant and animal death prior to the creation of Adam and Eve.

Answer: When a blade of grass loses its water content, turns brown, and ceases to grow, did it just die? Is that event due to Adam's sin? Is this the kind of death God was referring to when He told Adam, "for in the day that you eat of it, you shall surely die?"

The Bible clearly talks about 2 kinds of death. The first death is biologic. It involves the cessation of bodily functions: heartbeat, breathing, growing. Nearly all living things on this earth experience this first death (see below). The second death is a spiritual death. This death involves eternal separation from God (Rev 2:11, 20:6, 21.8). It is the result of rebellion against God and can only be avoided by being adopted into the family of God. Only humans can experience the second death as only humans have a spirit. The blade of grass that withers and decomposes is certainly not experiencing the second death.

Did biological death (the first death) exist on the earth prior to Adam and Eve's sin? The notion that all living things were eternal prior to "the fall" is widely taught throughout Christendom. It is not taught in Genesis. God never states that His biologic creations will not age or that they will live forever.

In fact, this can't be the case. Adam and Eve were told to eat from the plants in the garden. This involved the killing of plants and plant parts. Once ingested, anything that is still alive dies and is broken down into digestible chemicals. This would also be true for all other plant eating animals. Many of the dinosaurs were carnivores. They only ate other animals. Unless Adam sinned before any of the carnivorous animals ate their first meal (highly unlikely and certainly not indicated in the text of Genesis), then animals died being food for other animals. Natural Revelation tells us that this cycle of living organisms dying as food for other organisms occurred on a continuous basis over billions of years.

The fact that the first death existed prior to Adam's sin only clarifies what exactly God's judgement on Adam was for his disobedience. Adam's blatant disregard for God's command resulted in his being sentenced to the second death. An unimaginably horrible death since it involves eternally severing the relationship between 2 spiritual beings, God and man. This sentence would have been carried out had not God arranged for a Redeemer for Adam and his descendants.

This understanding of what kind of death God was referring to in Genesis 2:17 is also supported by the text, "in the day that you eat of it, you shall surely die." Adam did not experience biological death the day he disobeyed God. Adam lived to be over 900 years old so his biological death was far removed from that fateful day. Adam did experience the sentence of the second death on that fateful day. In Romans 6:23, Paul reiterates what was spoken of in Genesis. Sin results in the sentence of (the second) death. He cannot be talking about the first, biological death, since there are sinners who did not, or will not ever experience that death (Elijah - 2 Kings 2:11, Enoch - Gen 5:22, all those living when Jesus returns). The teaching that sin, which is not covered by the righteousness of Christ, condemns the sinner to eternal destruction (the second death), is a consistent and clear theme throughout Scripture. So, it is true that death - spiritual death - did not exist before Adam sinned. Biological death however, was built into God's system for renewing, sustaining, and recycling the building blocks of life.

Objection 2: *"Six days you shall labor and do all your work, but the seventh day is a Sabbath of the Lord your God... For in six days the Lord made the heavens and the earth, the sea and all that is in them, and rested on the seventh day; therefore the Lord blessed the Sabbath day and made it holy"* (Exodus 20:9,11).

Answer: The above verse clearly speaks of God making the *"heavens and the earth"* in *"six days"* and God resting on *"the seventh day."* This forms the basis of our seven day week. Our calendar could have been fashioned in all sorts of configurations, but it is, in fact, fashioned after the biblical seven-day creation "week." Surely this does not allow some alternate interpretation regarding how long God's creative work lasted?

The purpose of the Sabbath day, important enough that our honoring of the Sabbath was included in God's 10 commandments for His people, was to set aside a full day on a recurring basis to cease from our work in order to worship our Creator. God could have made this interval every other day, every 4th day, every 30th day or every 30th year. In His wisdom, He chose every 7th day. Exodus 20 relates this choice of a Sabbath every 7 days to God's work in creating the universe.

We saw earlier that the Hebrew word for "day," yom, can mean any defined period of time. What if Exodus 20:9,11 instead read, *"Six days you shall labor and do all your work, but the seventh day is a Sabbath to the Lord your God... For in six distinct eras the Lord created the heavens and the earth, the sea and all that is in them, and rested during the seventh; therefore the Lord has blessed the Sabbath day and made it holy."*

This translation wouldn't change the command. We would still have a 7-day week with the 7th day committed to worship. It also wouldn't change the underlying reasoning behind the grouping into 7. God created the universe in six defined periods of time and rested on the 7th. We are to mimic the same. For us, those periods are 24-hour days. For God, those periods were on a much grander scale. Although this does give "yom" a different meaning in adjacent verses, it is well within the bounds of translation and creates harmony with both Scripture and God's Natural Revelation.

The Christian church stands in danger of losing its credibility, much like it did in the 1600's. Our observations tell us that the sun is the center of our solar system. Our observations also tell us the earth is billions of years old and that life appeared on earth with a definite progression from simple to more complex. Countless persons have rejected the Bible as the inerrant Word of God due to the narrow interpretation by some of the creation account in Genesis 1. The Church needs to speak as one on this issue, aligning Special Revelation, the Bible, with Natural Revelation. The explanation of God's creative work detailed in this chapter brings harmony, consistency, and unity to all of God's Revelation.

6

Salvation

I remember being about 7 or 8, sitting in Sunday School, hearing a lesson about heaven. The teacher was telling us that the way we got to go to heaven was to believe in Jesus. I think the verse she was using was John 3:16: "For God so loved the world that He gave His only Son, that whoever believes in Him should not perish, but have eternal life." We needed to believe that Jesus was the son of God and that He died for our sins. It really didn't have anything to do with being good. We might hear others say that, but that wasn't correct. Faith in Jesus was the key.

Sometime after that, we were learning about Joseph and his family in the Old Testament. We heard about how his brothers sold him into slavery and how he ended up in Egypt; how he became a valued servant of an Egyptian government official, but was later thrown in jail for rebuffing a sexual advance. He remained faithful to God, however, and was blessed by becoming second only to Pharaoh. Surely Joseph was a man of God, someone we will meet in heaven someday. Or will we? Did Joseph believe in Jesus? Did he know that Jesus died for his sins? Hadn't I just been taught that faith in Jesus was necessary for anyone to go to heaven?

SALVATION

Some might think this was a childish or ridiculous thought. Jesus had not been revealed to Joseph, or anyone else living during Old Testament times, so they couldn't be expected to have faith in Him. Or could they? Maybe the answer was that these people needed to have faith in the promise of the Christ, the Holy One to come to redeem Israel. Maybe back then that's what led to salvation. I do believe that was what I was told when I asked my teacher what saved Joseph and his family. Was that correct?

This problem, the problem of explaining soteriology, or the "how" of salvation, for those who lived prior to the coming of Christ, is not a simple task. Christian theologians from different denominations argue about the "how" of salvation for those of us living now, *after* Christ's death and resurrection: What constitutes faith in Jesus? Why do some believe while other's don't? What is the Holy Spirit's role in bringing us to faith and keeping us from falling away? Is faith a gift of God given to us apart from anything we do or any other personal trait? Does the new birth come before faith or is it merely a reflection of our faith? And what about baptism? Does it play any role in our salvation? All these questions have been posed and most have been answered, albeit differently, depending on whether you are a Catholic or Baptist or Pentecostal Christian.

Does it matter? Honestly, most Christians don't bother trying to work out in their heads the spiritual details of how we are saved. It's so much simpler to just say that faith in Jesus as the Messiah, the Son of God who came to redeem His people, is what is needed for salvation. This is a true statement that every Christian can agree on (although we still may need to explain what "faith" means). Trying to answer all those other questions may just lead to arguments and bad feelings and fragmentation of the Body of Christ (sound familiar?).

I would suggest that the exploration of most of those questions should be left to those with a sincere interest in digging deeper into the Scriptures, and only then with a spirit of humility and a prior commitment to not let differences of opinion cause separation. We are called to be one in Christ (John 17). There are reasons to excommunicate persons from the Church or to break fellowship with a group teaching heresy, but disagreeing on when spiritual rebirth happens is not one of them.

But where does this leave our spiritual ancestors? How should we explain the salvation of Abraham, Isaac, and Jacob, let alone all the other people striving to follow God pre-Jesus?

There are at least 3 reasons why answering this question is important. First, the children of Israel were God's chosen people, chosen to bring God's law and His revelation to humanity. The story of Christianity really began with their lives and their experiences. Understanding God's provision for their salvation may help us better understand our own salvation.

Second, this is a relatively large group of people we are talking about. Certainly over a billion lived from the time God created man until the coming of Christ. Most of these people were not Jewish. Were they all lost? And what about the Jews who lived between Adam and Isaiah, before the giving of the more detailed prophesies of Jesus?

Third, most of the Bible, almost three-quarters of it, is Old Testament. To say that we don't really know what saved those who lived during this time period is to say we really don't understand three quarters of the Bible.

Biblical scholars have, over the years, devised various complex explanations. A prominent one divides history into specific time periods, or dispensations. Each of these dispensations represents a segment of time when God gave a piece of His revelation to the people, including rules to follow. When the people demonstrated their failure to keep these rules, which inevitably happened, God instituted another dispensation with new information and new rules. Those that were saved, were those that demonstrated a sincere desire to follow God's rules. The most common division splits all of human history into 7 segments:

1. Innocence - from creation of Adam to the Fall
2. Conscience - from the Fall to the Great Flood
3. Government - from the Flood to Abraham
4. Promise - from Abraham to Moses
5. Law - from Moses to Jesus
6. Grace - from Jesus to the rapture of the Church
7. Kingdom - the 1000 year reign of the Church on earth

Another somewhat related explanation is called Covenant Theology. This explanation divides history into different periods based on promises, or covenants, that God made with His people. In the big picture view there are 3 covenants, the Covenant of Works, the Covenant of Grace, and the Covenant of Redemption. The Covenant of Works was made with Adam and involved His obedience in return for life: *"From any tree of the garden you may eat freely, but from the tree of the knowledge of good and evil you shall not eat, for in the day that you eat from it you will surely die"* (Gen 2:16). This covenant lasted until Adam broke this command, recorded in Chapter 3 of Genesis. The actual duration of this covenant is not known. It could have lasted only hours or many years.

The Covenant of Grace is said to have begun with the promise of one who would come and crush Satan. In Gen 3:15 God says to Satan after successfully tempted Eve to sin, *"And I will put enmity between you and the woman, and between your seed and her seed; He shall bruise you on the head, and you shall bruise him on the heel."*

This promise is taken as the first prophecy about the coming of Jesus and His purpose on earth - to crush the power of Satan. The Covenant of Grace is further divided into individual covenants made with Noah, Abraham, Moses, and David. The covenant given to Moses included the giving of the Ten Commandments, all the laws regarding sacrifices, and the recurring promise, *"I will be your God and you will be my people."*

The Covenant of Redemption was the agreement made between God the Father and God the Son regarding the incarnation, death, and resurrection of Jesus, required to redeem, or buy back, a people for His eternal kingdom. Those that adhere to Covenant Theology generally teach that salvation in the Old Testament came through faith in a promised Messiah.

There are other explanations, most variations on these two themes, including Dual-covenant theology, Progressive dispensationalism, New Covenant theology, and Supersessionism. Unfortunately, all of these suffer from a couple of troubling problems.

First, Jesus came to earth bringing a New Covenant (Luk 22:20, 2 Cor 3:6, Heb 9:15) that was foretold in Jeremiah 31:

> *"Behold, days are coming," declares the Lord, "when I will make a new covenant with the house of Israel and with the house of Judah" (v 31).*

If this was the Covenant of Grace, then it was not a New Covenant at all. However, if the New Covenant was that faith in Jesus, the Son of God, brings salvation to all those who believe, then this was not the covenant for those living before the incarnation of Christ. Salvation must have been made available

SALVATION

to those *before* the coming of this New Covenant by some other means.

Second, both Dispensationalism and Covenant theology make it sound like God changed the rules as He went. During period X one set of expectations were in effect, while in period Y another set of expectations were delivered to the people and monitored for adherence. Also, many people's lives spanned 2 separate periods, whether using the Dispensational schema or the Covenantal one. For example, Noah lived during both the Age of Conscience and the Age of Government. Which rules applied to Noah?

Third, by saying that people living in the Old Testament period were saved by their faith in a Messiah who had yet to come, we are assuming that the word about this Messiah was faithfully transmitted from generation to generation. The promise of Gen 3:15, *"he* [her seed] *will bruise your head,"* wasn't even given to Adam and Eve, but to Satan. It was written down for us by Moses in about 1500 BC, thousands of years after it was initially said. We don't know if Adam and Eve even heard this prophecy. There is no evidence that it was ever repeated to anyone after it was initially uttered by God. No one living between Adam and Moses ever spoke of a coming Redeemer or Messiah.

It seems highly unlikely that faith in a coming Messiah was the criteria for salvation when it was spoken of only once prior to the writings of the prophet Isaiah around 700 BC, and that one utterance occurred in the Garden of Eden in a somewhat cryptic statement made by God whilst cursing a serpent. The prophetic allusions to Jesus found in earlier writings such as the Psalms are clear in hindsight, but certainly would not have been understood as prophesies at the time of their writing.

So, if faith in Jesus, or a yet-to-be-revealed Jesus, was not what saved people before His arrival, what did? What does Scripture say about salvation prior to the coming of Christ? There is certainly no John 3:16 of the Old Testament; "If you do this, or believe this, you will be saved." That would make this discussion short.

The word "salvation" appears in the Old Testament in 108 verses. Sixty-one of those verses are in Psalms and another 25 in Isaiah. A handful of verses use "salvation" to describe God rescuing His people from earthly harm or danger. In Exodus 14, Moses says to the children of Israel as they are fleeing Egypt, *"Do not fear! Stand by and see the salvation of the Lord which He will accomplish for you today"* (v 13). David likewise talks about God's salvation in His song of praise for protection from Saul: *"My God, my rock, in whom I take refuge, my shield and the horn of my salvation, my stronghold and my refuge; my savior, you save me from violence"* (2 Sam 22:3). In 2 Chronicles, Jahaziel says to those living in Judah, readying for a battle, *"You need not fight in this battle; station yourselves, stand and see the salvation of the Lord on your behalf"* (20:1).

Most of the verses, however, identify God as the source of our salvation or give thanks to God for His salvation. Some representative verses from the Psalms:

Psalm 3:8: *Salvation belongs to the Lord; your blessing be upon the people.*

Psalm 13:5: *But I have trusted in your lovingkindness; My heart shall rejoice in your salvation.*

Psalm 18:46: *The Lord lives, and blessed be my rock; And exalted be the God of my salvation.*

SALVATION

Psalm 25:5: *Lead me in your truth and teach me, for you are the God of my salvation.*

Psalm 38:22: *Make haste to help me, O Lord, my salvation.*

These verses demonstrate a clear understanding that salvation comes from God. They also indicate an expectation that salvation will come to those who are writing these verses, though Psalm 27:9 lets us know it is not assured: *Do not hide your face from me, do not turn your servant away in anger; you have been my help; do not abandon me nor forsake me; O God of my salvation.*

Isaiah similarly identifies God as the source of salvation. Isaiah 12:2 states, *"Behold, God is my salvation, I will trust and not be afraid; for the Lord God is my strength and song, and He has become my salvation."* Isaiah 25:9 says, *"Behold, this is our God for whom we have waited that He might save us. This is the Lord for whom we have waited; let us rejoice and be glad in His salvation."*

For whom was this salvation intended? For everyone? For the Jews only? For those who were obedient to the law of God?

About a dozen verses give us some sense about who qualified for God's salvation. In the midst of trying to understand his suffering, Job said,

Though He slay me, I will hope in Him. Nevertheless I will argue my ways before Him. This also will be my salvation, for a Godless man may not come before His presence (Job 13:15,16).

David stated, *"But the salvation of the righteous is from the Lord; He is their strength in time of trouble"* (Ps 37:39).

In Psalm 50 we read, *"He who offers a sacrifice of thanksgiving honors Me; and to him who orders his way aright, to him I shall show the salvation of God"* (v 23). In Psalm 85:9 the Psalmist says, *"Surely His salvation is near to them who fear Him."* Psalm 118 says, *"The sound of joyful shouting and salvation is in the tents of the righteous; the right hand of the Lord does valiantly"* (v 15).

Salvation was granted to those who fear God and who were deemed "righteous." But how was this righteousness obtained? One possible answer to this would be through obedience to the law. God delivered many laws and rules of conduct to His people through the prophets. He certainly did this with an expectation that they would at least try to follow them. Maybe the degree to which people strove to follow these rules determined whether they were considered "righteous" by God. Of course we know from Genesis 3 that the very first command given to the first humans was quickly disobeyed. We also know that God's people made a habit of breaking God's laws (e.g. the golden calf debacle, Jonah refusing to go to Nineveh, King David arranging the death of Uriah). Given the intricacies of the law, it would be a stretch to think that anyone could have earned the title of "righteous."

In the 7th Century BC, Isaiah uttered a profound and prophetic statement regarding this required righteousness:

> *I will rejoice greatly in the Lord, my soul will exult in my God; For He has clothed me with garments of salvation, He has wrapped me with a robe of righteousness. As a bridegroom decks himself with a garland, and as a bride adorns herself with her jewels. (Is 61:10)*

Isaiah tells us that God not only grants us salvation, He somehow gives us the needed righteousness. But on what basis?

SALVATION

The answer to the question of how righteousness was obtained before Christ came was misunderstood by most Jews. In order to clarify this, the Apostle Paul spent the first four chapters of his letter to the Romans walking them through the issue. He starts by stating that the existence of God and His majesty has always been clearly seen by observing the creation (Rom 1:20). But, even though people knew God, they chose to not honor God or give thanks to Him (1:21). Therefore, God allowed them to follow their passions which resulted in rampant evil: strife, envy, murder, sexual sin, greed and arrogance (1:24-32).

At this point, the Jews who are listening to Paul are nodding their head in agreement. Paul knows that they are thinking to themselves, "Those lawless pagans. They cheat, steal, and lie. They practice sexual immorality. They have crooked banking practices. They do not honor God by observing the festivals and Sabbaths. God will surely take His vengeance on them."

Then, Paul does the unexpected. He turns and looks straight into his fellow Jews' eyes and points the finger of condemnation squarely at them.

> *Therefore you have no excuse, every one of you who passes judgement, for in that which you judge another, you condemn yourself. For you who judge practice the same things.* (2:1)

Not exactly what the Jews wanted to hear. Paul spends the rest of chapter 2 blasting their thoughts of self-righteousness.

> *But do you suppose this, O man, when you pass judgement on those who practice such things and do the same yourself, that you will escape the judgement of God* (2:3)?

Having the law doesn't necessarily mean following the law,

nor does it provide any protection from judgement: *"For all who have sinned without the law will also perish without the law, and all who have sinned under the law will be judged by the law; for it is not hearers of the law who are just before God but the doers of the law will be justified"* (2:12,13).

Paul continues his diatribe against his fellow Jews' hubris by calling out their specific sins:

> *But if you bear the name 'Jew' and rely upon the law and boast in God and know His will and approve the things that are essential, being instructed out of the law, and are confident that you yourself are a guide to the blind, a light to those who are in darkness, a corrector of the foolish, a teacher of the immature, having in the law an embodiment of knowledge and of the truth, you, therefore, who teach another, do you not teach yourself? You who preach that one shall not steal, do you steal? You who say that one should not commit adultery, do you commit adultery? You who abhor idols, do you rob temples? You who boast in the law, through your breaking the law, do you dishonor God (2:17-23)?*

Nor does being circumcised (carrying the sign of being a descendent of Abraham) afford any benefit to those who break the law. *"For indeed circumcision is of value if you practice the law; but if you are a transgressor of the law, your circumcision has become uncircumcision"* (2:25).

Paul systematically takes the legs out from under any argument the Jews would have for being superior to the Gentiles.

Next, Paul makes clear that no Jew, or non-Jew for that matter, has kept the law:

SALVATION

What then? Are we better than they? Not at all; for we have already charged that both Jews and Greeks are all under sin; as it is written, "There is none righteous, not even one; there is none who understands, there is none who seeks for God; all have turned aside, together they have become useless; there is none who does good, no not even one" (3:9-12).

He sums up this section with the inevitable conclusion: *"by the works of the law no flesh will be justified* [declared righteous] *in His sight"* (v 20).

Very bad news for those who thought their righteousness, and thus their salvation, came from participation in all the sacrifices, Sabbath laws, and dietary observances.

So, if righteousness, and salvation, didn't come from following the rules, where did it come from? Paul announces the good news meant for all people:

Now, *"apart from the law the righteousness of God has been manifested, being witnessed by the law and the prophets, even the righteousness of God through faith in Jesus Christ for all those who believe; for there is no distinction; for all have sinned and fall short of the glory of God, being justified as a gift by His grace through the redemption which is in Christ Jesus" (3:21-24).*

Praise be to God for providing a path to righteousness for all who have faith in Jesus.

But this still doesn't answer the question of Abraham, Isaac, and Jacob's righteousness. We live in the post-Jesus era. We have the witness of the apostles and the last 2000 years of history. They did not. Paul addresses this next,

What then shall we say that Abraham, our forefather according to the flesh, has found? For if Abraham was justified by works, he has something to boast about, but not before God. For it is written, "Abraham believed God and it was credited to him as righteousness" (4:1-3).

Abraham *believed* God. That was the key to being *"wrapped in the robe of righteousness."* The Old Testament reference used here by Paul comes from Gen 15. God had just told a childless, old Abraham that His descendants shall be in number like the stars in the sky. Abraham could have scoffed. He could have said, "I know you are God, creator of the universe, but what you are promising is a bit ridiculous." He did not. He believed God and it was credited to him as righteousness.

It is important to note that Abraham's righteousness was granted not only due to his belief *in God*, but also because of his belief *in the promises of God*. Later in chapter 4, Paul makes this point more plainly:

In hope against hope he [Abraham] *believed, so that he might become a father of many nations according to that which had been spoken, 'So shall your descendants be.' Without becoming weak in faith he contemplated his own body, now as good as dead since he was about a hundred years old, and the deadness of Sarah's womb; yet, with respect to the promise of God, he did not waver in unbelief, but grew strong in faith, giving glory to God, and being fully assured that what God had promised He was able also to perform. Therefore it was also credited to him as righteousness (4:18-22).*

Why not just say Abraham was credited with righteousness by belief *in God*? Why also add *in the promises of God*? It turns out this is vitally important.

There are many people, and beings, that believe in God, the creator of the universe, but who do not accept the promises of God. Pharaoh, after enduring the many plagues on Egypt, believed in God, but he never accepted his promises. The Israelites who left Egypt believed in God, but did not believe His promise that He would assure their possession of the promised land. None were allowed entry. In our present day, those who follow Islam believe in God, a God who created the universe. They identify Him as the God of Abraham. Yet they do not believe His promise of one who would come to be *"pierced through for our transgressions,"* and *"crushed for our iniquities"* (Is 53:5). Conversely, imagine what the outcome would have been for an Israelite in Egypt who didn't believe the promise of God that He would kill the firstborn of those who did not put lamb's blood on their doorpost. They might truly believe *in* God, but just not think He would do such a thing. The result of that unbelief would have been a child's death.

Belief in the promises of God is synonymous with trust. Belief "in" someone, means you accept statements about who that person is.

"George Washington was the first president of the United States." Either you believe that or not. You don't trust that GW was the first president. Trust implies you are putting something at risk based on a belief. I believe that my financial advisor is smart and has my best interest in mind, thus I am willing to trust him to invest my retirement funds. Abraham trusted in God's promise that he would be the "father of many nations" to the extent that he was willing to kill the promised heir, Isaac, if God told him to. Abraham trusted that God would raise Isaac from the dead, if needed, to fulfil that promise (Heb 11:17-19). Belief and trust together define the Bible's use of the word "faith."

The remarkable point to all of the preceding discussion in this chapter, and the reason to so carefully ascertain the source of righteousness in the Old Testament, is that the criteria for salvation in the New Testament is exactly the same as it has been since the beginning of humanity - belief in God and the promises of God! The rules of the game have not changed. God is the same yesterday, today and forever (Mal 3:6, Heb 13:8). This is the unifying, overarching, unchanging requirement for salvation.

What then is the Old Covenant and what is the New Covenant and how do they fit into God's timeless plan for salvation?

The Old Covenant primarily involved the promises God gave in regards to the use of animal sacrifices to atone for the sins of the people. The required and truly effective sacrifice for sin, the life and death of Jesus, was to occur in the future. Prior to His arrival, God provided a temporary means for obtaining forgiveness. This involved the shedding of animals' blood. God promised that these sacrifices would atone for the sins of the people, and they did. It was not that the blood of bulls and goats had any real power to pay for human sin (Heb 10:4), rather it was faith in God's promises that made the sacrifices efficacious.

The New Covenant, or the new promise of God, is that faith in Jesus of Nazareth, the Son of God, who came to be the real and final sacrifice for sin, is now the source of our righteousness (Phl 3:9). No longer are people to sacrifice animals and believe that their blood provides any benefit. Those days of daily sacrifice were meant to point to this day. Faith in the person of Jesus, and the shedding of His blood, are the means of our forgiveness (1 Jn 1:7).

After Jesus shared the Last Supper with His disciples, He lifted a glass of wine and said, "This cup is the New Covenant in

My blood" (1 Cor 11:25). The key word in this sentence is not "blood"; the Jews were very familiar with the shedding of blood. Animal blood was all over the temple. The key word in this sentence is "My." "My blood." Jesus' blood was the required ingredient for the salvation of mankind, not animal's blood. The New Covenant is superior to the Old Covenant since faith is now to be directed at the true source of our redemption, Jesus, not a symbol or shadow of that source (Heb 8:1-6).

In the New Covenant era, belief in God means believing in the newly revealed triune, or three part, nature of God. Most importantly, it means believing what Jesus said about Himself. He is the Messiah (Jn 4:26). He is the Son of God (Lk 22:70). He has the power to forgive sin (Mk 2:10). He is the way, the truth and the light. No one can come to [God] the Father, but through Him (Jn 14:6). He is one with the Father (Jn 10:30). He is the judge over humanity (Jn 5:22).

The Apostle Paul tells us that in Him, Jesus, *"the fullness of Deity dwells in bodily form"* (Col 2:9). John completes this description of Jesus being God by informing us that Jesus was present at the beginning of time and everything was created by Him (Jn 1:1-3).

God the Son, Jesus, was fully human and fully divine. Jesus' humanity was evident by His bodily form; His experience of the full range of human emotion; the fact that he experienced hunger, thirst, and pain; the fact that he was tempted in all ways just as we are; and the observation that he bled and died.

The coexistence of God and man in one being is supernatural - beyond human reason. Explanations of how Jesus accomplished this are inherently irrational. Some have tried to make sense of it by theorizing that He only appeared human or that His divinity came and went.[1] Scripture, however, is clear on this issue. Our inability to describe *how* Jesus was both fully God and fully man does not change the glorious truth that He was both human and Divine.

In the New Testament era, belief in the promises of God means trusting that God the Father, and God the Son, will do those things They say They will do. This includes blessing those who believe Jesus' claims about Himself by hearing their prayer, sending the Spirit to dwell within them, clothing them in God's righteousness, and granting them eternal life. It also includes Jesus' promise to return to earth in the future, to raise the dead, and to sit as judge over all humanity.

Jesus has promised to gather the righteous to Himself to live in a new heaven and a new earth. He has promised to condemn all those who are not clothed in the righteousness of Christ to eternal destruction. Other New Covenant promises regarding prayer, confession, the Lord's Supper, and baptism (discussed in later chapters) are a source of spiritual comfort, freedom from guilt, and heartfelt thanksgiving.

Salvation is a gift of God. In His mercy, He created a way for humankind to obtain the righteousness that He requires apart from perfect obedience. Belief and trust in Him has been the criteria for receiving His righteousness from the beginning. The coming of Jesus, the promised Messiah, did not change this formula. Rather, it provided an opportunity for people to demonstrate their trust in His ancient promises. Praise be to the Father for providing the Lamb of God who purchased us with His very own blood.

This explanation of God's provision for man's salvation since the time of their creation is biblically accurate, harmonizes the texts of both the Old and New Testaments, and provides a

SALVATION

consistent view of God's intervention in human affairs throughout human history.

7

Baptism: Its Meaning and Importance

Disagreements over the meaning and practice of baptism have existed in the Christian church since the early years of the Reformation. Questions about who, when, how, and why have been debated, argued, and written about extensively. As the dust settled on all the controversy, 2 distinct camps arose explaining the meaning of baptism: the baptism as a "sign" camp and the baptism as a "bridge" camp. Major denominations that belong to the baptism as a "sign" camp include Methodists, Presbyterians, Episcopalians, and Adventists. Orthodox Christians, Catholics, Lutherans, and those in the Church of Christ belong to the "bridge" camp.

When most people think of the word "sign", they think of a large, flat surface with something written on it that either tells you what to do (Stop, Yield, don't go over 50 mph) or provides some sort of information (buy this product, next street is Washington St, State Park in 5 miles). In the context of baptism, the word "sign" is used as something that represents something else. A reasonable analogy is the gold ring that some people wear on their left 4th finger. This ring is a "sign" that the person wearing it has experienced something special, in this case a marriage. The ring is not the marriage nor does wearing such a ring necessarily mean that the person is married. Anyone can put a gold ring on their 4th left finger. Yet, it is generally recognized that those bearing this sign claim something for themselves. It is a sign of belonging, love, and commitment.

For those in the "sign" camp, baptism likewise has its meaning rooted in a visible display of a background reality. Baptism was instituted (so the "sign" camp would say) to remind us that by the shedding of His blood, our sins are washed away; that through faith, we are buried with Him and thus will rise again, just as He was; and that we (the baptized) are the recipients of all the promises made to those that belong to Him. The baptism in no way accomplishes or facilitates any of these things, rather, the baptism serves as a visible sign, a reminder, that these promises are true. This explanation of the meaning of baptism does not violate either of the 2 essentials of Christianity, i.e. belief that Jesus is the Messiah, the Son of God, and trust that we are saved by faith in His sacrificial death on our behalf. Thus, this is one possible explanation.

The "bridge" group has a distinctly different understanding of baptism. A bridge is a structure that unites 2 previously separated entities. It joins them in such a way that the transfer of items from one to the other can occur freely and the 2 once separate entities can now call themselves one. Baptism (so the "bridge" camp would say) actually builds a bridge between God and the person baptized, facilitating the flow of God's Grace into the life of the one baptized. This Grace includes the forgiveness of sins, the gift of the Holy Spirit, and the incorporation of the baptized into the family of God - the Church. Unlike those in the "sign" camp that insist that the act of baptism in no way results in any significant changes in the spiritual status of a person, those in the "bridge" camp claim that the act of baptism results in extraordinary spiritual changes. This explanation of the meaning of baptism also does not violate the belief that Jesus is the Messiah, the Son of God. The "bridge" camp claims it does not violate trusting that we are saved by faith in His sacrificial death on our behalf. If this claim is in fact true then this is another possible explanation.

These two explanations of the meaning of baptism are mutually exclusive and thus both can't be true at the same time. Of course, neither could be true, but given that these are the two main explanations for baptism that currently exist in the Church, we should consider them both in light of Scripture.

Interestingly, if we were to poll the current Christian church for its opinion on this topic, based on numbers of adherents, the "bridge" camp would win. Approximately 1.4 billion of the 2 billion persons who confess Christ as Lord and Savior see baptism as a powerful, spiritually active event in the life of a Christian. Many Protestants are not aware of this. Secondly, if we were to ask which explanation the Church has held the longest, again the "bridge" camp would prevail. The understanding of baptism as an event that results in forgiveness of sins and entry into the Body of Christ was the sole teaching of the Church until roughly 500 years ago. Another often unknown fact. But, neither of these justifications (majority rule or longevity rule) determines truth. The truth needs to come from Scripture and so to Scripture we shall turn to see which explanation is supported by God's Words of Life.

When it comes to New Testament passages addressing the meaning of baptism, there are 9 verses appearing in 8 different books which use the word "baptism" (Gr, baptismo) in the context of a ceremonial washing performed in the name of the Father, Son, and Holy Spirit. There are another 4 or so that imply Christian baptism by their mention of water or washing, but given the contentious nature of their interpretation, we will hold these for later consideration and step through the former passages in their order of appearance, specifically considering if they support the "sign" view of baptism or the "bridge" view.[1]

BAPTISM: ITS MEANING

1. *Matthew 28:19: Go therefore and make disciples of all the nations, baptizing them in the name of the Father and the Son and the Holy Spirit, teaching them to observe all that I have commanded you.*

On the surface, this passage, which serves as the blueprint for Christian baptism, may not appear to speak to either the "sign" or "bridge" view of baptism. But a few thoughts are pertinent. First, baptism is apparently an integral part of making disciples. It is mentioned first as part of the 2 activities that the Holy Spirit tells us are needed to "make disciples" of all nations. Baptism must be quite important to God given this emphasis. Second, the baptism spoken of in this passage is distinctly different than the baptism the Jews were accustomed to, that is, the baptism of John. That baptism was a "baptism of repentance" and was not done in the name of anyone. This new baptism was to be done "in the name of" the triune God, or more accurately, "into (Gr, eis) the name of" the triune God.

This subtle but important distinction is lost on most of us as this figure of speech is not used in our present day. In Greek culture, at the time of this writing, the figure of speech "into the name of" indicated creating a legal association between the person being pledged into the name of the other. An example of this, other than baptism, was when a transfer of real estate was to take place. The piece of land was entered "into the name of (so and so)" in the official ledger. An ownership relationship was thus created. By being baptized "into the name of" the triune God, we place ourselves under His loving authority and become one of His cherished possessions.

So which explanation is best represented by this passage? Given the importance assigned to baptism and the language of legal association used, it seems something more than a "sign" or remembrance is indicated. The linking together as in a "bridge" is not expressly stated, but seems implied.

> 2. *Mark 16:16: He that believes and is baptized will be saved, he that believes not will be damned.*

This short and to the point verse is remarkable for its linking of faith and baptism together as criteria for salvation. There are many other places in Scripture where faith is listed alone as the criteria for salvation, however these verses must be considered along with Mark 16:16 to formulate a complete understanding of salvation. Passages cannot be dismissed or ignored because they don't seem to fit one's soteriology. Rather, one's soteriology needs to be able to incorporate all the pertinent passages in a way that brings harmony to all of Scripture.

No more will be said at this point about this verse, other than to note the implausible notion that God would link an event that is purely symbolic, without any power to cause real spiritual change, to salvation. This dual criteria of belief and baptism for salvation that is so clearly and simply stated by the Holy Spirit through Mark's pen seems to point to something other than a mere ceremonial remembrance of promises.

> 3. *Acts 2:38-39: And Peter said to them, "Repent, and each of you be baptized in the name of Jesus Christ for the forgiveness of your sins; and you will receive the gift of the Holy Spirit. For the promise is for you and your children and for all who are far off, as many as the Lord will call unto himself.*

This verse comes immediately after Peter's Pentecostal teaching to those who witnessed the apostles of Christ speaking

BAPTISM: ITS MEANING

in many different languages. These Jewish men were "pierced to the heart" (Acts 2:37) after learning that the recently crucified Jesus was indeed the Messiah. They asked, "What shall we do" (v 37)? Peter's answer is a bit astounding: repent and be baptized. No penance, no offering of an animal sacrifice (the usual and traditional way to obtain forgiveness for a sin), no mourning or application of sackcloth and ashes. Instead, these men were told to renounce their former ways (repent) and to undergo baptism "into (Gr, eis) the name of Jesus Christ." They were not told to do this as a sign of allegiance or remembrance. It was to be done "for the forgiveness of your sins."

The language in this verse couldn't be clearer. We saw in Mark 16:16 a linking of baptism to salvation. In this verse we are told what baptism is for - it is for the forgiveness of sins. Perhaps, that is the reason, or at least one of the reasons, for the placement of baptism alongside belief in Mark 16:16. Forgiveness is an integral part of being made clean in God's sight. The promise of the gift of the Holy Spirit is also linked to baptism in this verse, although not in such a direct fashion. The gift of the Spirit is spoken of as a natural consequence of the repentance and baptism.

Peter's teaching in this verse indicates that those who participate in baptism receive direct spiritual benefits. The baptism results in forgiveness and the promise of the Spirit. Many Protestant denominations have denied these benefits of baptism (we shall explore some of the reasons later), while Catholic and Orthodox Christians have always joyfully embraced these blessings. This explanation of what baptism is for is not consistent with the "sign" understanding of baptism. Baptism appears to act as a conduit or "bridge" for receiving God's gracious gifts of forgiveness and the Spirit.

4. *Acts 22:16: And now why do you delay? Arise, and be baptized, and wash away your sins, calling on His name.*

It is very helpful, and in many cases essential, in pinning down the correct meaning of a verse to have parallel, or similar verses saying the same thing in a slightly different way. Acts 22:16 does just that. These words were spoken to the Apostle Paul 3 days after he was blinded by the light of Christ on the road to Damascus. Ananias, a disciple of Jesus, is instructed by the Spirit to shepherd Paul (at that time called Saul) in the immediate aftermath of his dramatic encounter with Jesus. After placing his hands on Paul and restoring his sight, he says to him *"And now why do you delay? Arise, and be baptized, and wash away your sins, calling on His name."*

Once again we see that the result of being baptized is the removal of sin, confirming the answer to the "What's baptism for?" question addressed in Acts 2:38. To make the association with baptism even clearer, in this verse the Spirit uses the phrase "and *wash away your sin.*" Baptism is a ceremonial washing - the application of water is required. When Ananias says these words to Paul, Paul can only interpret them one way: I need to get up and be baptized in order to have my sins removed. The language of the verse points directly to baptism as the means by which Paul's sins will be taken away.

What gives baptism this supernatural power? Acts 22:16 tells us. The physical act of being washed is not enough. Calling on Jesus in faith, *"calling on His name"*, is what gives baptism its power and effectiveness. The act of baptism, done in the name of Jesus, with faith, channels God's forgiveness to the one being baptized. There is no "sign" of God's favor described in this verse. Ananias proclaims to Paul a real, spiritual benefit derived from being baptized.

BAPTISM: ITS MEANING

5. *Romans 6:3-4: Or do you not know that all of us who have been baptized into Christ Jesus have been baptized into His death? Therefore we have been buried with Him through baptism into death, in order that as Christ was raised from the dead through the glory of the Father, so we too might walk in newness of life.*

Romans 6 opens with Paul appealing to the Roman Christians regarding their lifestyle choices. He has just explained to them the truth that although one man, Adam, brought sin into the world and through him all men were made sinners, yet through Christ, the righteous One, all men who have faith in Him will be justified, that is, declared righteous before God. This however, is not to be viewed as a reason to be complacent about sin. Paul says in verse 1, *"What shall we say then? Are we to continue in sin so grace may abound?"* He answers himself in verse 2: *"May it never be! How shall we who died to sin still live in it?"*

Paul then follows this with an explanation of what this "died to sin" means: *"Or do you not know that all of us who have been baptized into Christ Jesus have been baptized into His death?"*

Wow! How many churches tell those who are about to be baptized that being baptized into Christ includes being baptized into His death? I've been to many baptisms in many different churches and have yet to hear these words. Paul goes on,

Therefore we have been buried with Him through baptism into death, in order that as Christ was raised from the dead through the glory of the Father, so we too might walk in newness of life. (6:4)

There it is again - *"buried with Him into death."* So baptism not only results in forgiveness of sins (Acts 2:38 and Acts 22:16), it also links us in some way to Christ's death and burial.

This is purely symbolic language, isn't it? Picture language meant to remind us of what Christ did for us, but not meant to convey a spiritual transformation. I mean, how can this ceremonial washing cause us to be *"buried with Him?"* We certainly have not been physically buried with Him.

Yet, the Spirit of God tells us in this passage that our baptism plays a significant role in our ability to say no to sin. Look again at how this verse starts. *"Do you not know?"* Apparently at least some of those he was speaking to didn't know, or Paul wouldn't have had to say this.

Do *we* know? Do we know that we have died to sin by being baptized into Christ's death? Since we have been buried with Christ *"through baptism,"* just as Christ was raised from the dead, we too have been raised to walk in newness of life, free from the bondage of sin. There is a clear teaching here that baptism facilitates this "newness of life."

Baptism changes us by spiritually binding us to Christ's death. How this burial "into His death" works is a mystery that is not explained. But Romans 6:3 and 4 is all about Paul reminding the disciples of Christ that their baptism resulted in a life-changing, life-empowering connection with our Redeemer.

> 6. *I Cor 12:13: For by one Spirit we were all baptized into one body, whether Jews or Greeks, whether slave or free, and we were all made to drink of one Spirit.*

Chapter 12 of First Corinthians is all about our unity as followers of Christ despite our apparent diversity. One and the same Spirit is responsible for our varied gifts (v 4), varied ministries (v 5) and varied contributions to the whole (v 6). This diversity creates the body of Christ, a divinely orchestrated group of people working together to build the Kingdom of God.

In 1 Cor 12:13, we are told that *"we were all baptized into (Gr, eis) one body."* What body is this?

The Apostle Paul uses the term "body" 18 times in chapter 12. His use of this word is consistent. The "body" that we are baptized into is that group of people who have the Spirit of God living and working in their lives. This is the Church. To drive home that point, Paul closes the chapter by affirming, *"Now you are Christ's body, and individually members of it. And God has appointed in the church first apostles, second prophets, third teachers, ..."* (vv 27,28).

So, we Christians *"were all baptized into one body"*, the Body of Christ, the Church. This phrase strongly implies that before being baptized, we were not part of the body. It would make no sense for Paul to tell us we were baptized *into* one Body, the Church, if we were already a part of that Body prior to baptism. Consider the case of someone being inducted into a sports Hall of Fame when they were already in the Hall of Fame. That makes no sense. Nor would Paul's teaching that we are baptized into the Body, if we were a part of that Body before baptism. This tells us that baptism is the official, ceremonial entry point into the family of God as an adopted child.[2]

This understanding of baptism as the "initiation rite," the event marking a change of status for those wanting to be disciples of Christ, was the teaching of the Church for the first 1500 years of its existence. It wasn't until the Protestant reformation, and its emphasis on "faith alone", that the efficacy of baptism was questioned. But, Scripture did not change during that period of reformation, nor any time since, and we are left with the words of Paul to the Corinthians. He reminds them that they were *"baptized into one body."* We must decide if Paul is telling us that a change actually occurred during baptism, or if Paul is using that phrase in some other symbolic way.

Looking back at the passages we have considered so far, the interpretation that baptism officially admits us into the Church would be consistent with the verses stating that baptism is linked to salvation, that it results in forgiveness of sins, and that we are baptized into Christ's death in order that we may live a new life.

(For those Protestants completely offended at this point based on "faith alone" grounds, please read on.)

> 7. Gal 3:26-27: *For you are all sons of God through faith in Christ Jesus. For all of you who were baptized into Christ have clothed yourselves with Christ.*

In this verse, Paul reminds the Galatians that they are *"all sons of God through faith in Christ Jesus."* What a glorious truth! He doesn't stop there, however. He adds some information about *how (*or possibly *when?)* this occurred. *"For all of you who were baptized into Christ have clothed yourselves with Christ."* Paul ties these two facts together in a way that makes them difficult to separate. Many Christian churches teach the first part of this passage, but not the second.

Understanding the meaning of *"clothed yourselves with Christ,"* as used in this verse, is essential if we are to make the correct link. Paul tells the Galatian church that being *"baptized into (Gr, eis) Christ"* means that they have been clothed with Christ. This "clothing" action is certainly connected with both baptism and *"faith in Christ Jesus."*

This being "clothed" could mean that we take on or display the characteristics of Christ: love, joy, peace, patience. In this sense, being clothed with Christ would have more of a "sign" meaning, similar to being clothed with your favorite team's logos and colors. People see you are a fan if you wear their clothing. They know that you identify with that group, concern yourself with how they do, and spend time watching and enjoying their activities. Being clothed with Christ could likewise mean we identify with Christ, concern ourselves with His teaching, and try to be like Him.

Alternately, being clothed with Christ could have a deeper meaning. How is this phrase used elsewhere in Scripture?

In the New Testament, the word "clothed" occurs 25 times, with 19 of them referring to something physically worn by a person (ie. linen, robes, purple). Two verses in Revelations refer to beings being clothed in "clouds" and "the sun," descriptions of what physically and visually surrounded them. The other three verses are likely more applicable to Gal 3:27.

In Luke 24:29, Jesus instructs His disciples *"I am sending forth the promise of my Father upon you; but you are to stay in the city until you are clothed with power from on high."*

This *"promise of my Father"* is the same promise spoken of by Peter in Acts 2:38 - the Spirit of God. The Spirit will clothe the disciples with power. What did this look like? Being clothed with power enabled the disciples to speak in the languages of all those in attendance at Pentecost, and to manifest the other gifts of the Spirit (prophesying, healing, teaching). Being "clothed with power" meant that the power of the Spirit became a part of the disciples and changed them from within so that they were able to do things they couldn't do before.

The other two verses are in 2 Cor 5. Here Paul is contrasting our current earthly existence with our future heavenly home. He refers to our physical body as our "earthly tent" or "house" and laments, *"For indeed in this house we groan, longing to be clothed with our dwelling in heaven."* (v2) He goes on,

> *"For indeed while we are in this tent, we groan, being burdened, because we do not want to be unclothed but to be clothed, so that what is mortal will be swallowed up by life." (v4)*

To be *"clothed with our dwelling in heaven"* means for us to be a part of heaven. For our mortal bodies, and lives, to be fundamentally transformed by Christ into our immortal heavenly bodies.

So we see that Paul's meaning of the word "clothed," when it is used in a spiritual context, means to be changed; to be transformed by the thing we are clothed with. In Gal 3:27, being *"clothed with Christ"* means to have Christ come into our life, melting our heart of stone, giving us a new heart, willing and able to live in accordance with the guidance of the Spirit (Ez 11:19). It is our adoption as "sons of God." This represents the fulfillment of the prophecy in Isaiah 61:10, *"I will rejoice greatly in the LORD, My soul will exult in my God; For He has clothed me with garments of salvation, He has wrapped me with a robe of righteousness."* Surely Christ is our garment of salvation!

> 8. *Col 2:11-12: And in Him you were also circumcised with a circumcision made without hands, in the removal of the body of the flesh by the circumcision of Christ; having been buried with Him in baptism, in which you were also raised up with Him through faith in the working of God, who raised Him from the dead.*

BAPTISM: ITS MEANING

In Col 2:11-12, the Holy Spirit presents another aspect of the meaning of baptism, namely its relation to circumcision. For over 2000 years, the Children of God had been performing this surgical procedure on their men and boys, down to the age of 8 days, in obedience to the command of God (Gen 17). What was this all about? Why would God ask for this to be done on every male that desired to become a "son of Abraham"? In the present day, this procedure is done with anesthesia, and if not done in the first few months of life, it's done in the operating room. It is painful. There is some risk of bleeding and infection.

When the command to circumcise all males was given to Abraham, God told *him "And you shall be circumcised in the flesh of your foreskin, and it shall be the sign of the covenant between me and you"* (Gen 17:11). We see that the primary meaning of circumcision was as the sign of the covenant. What covenant was this?

The first 8 verses of Genesis 17 lay out the multiple promises of God to Abraham which comprise this covenant. These include being made *"exceedingly fruitful"* (v 6), and the *"father of a multitude of nations"* (v 5), the promise that *"kings will come forth from you"* (v 6), and the pledge to give to Abraham and his descendants the land of Canaan (v 8). Lastly, was the life giving promise *"to be God to you and to your descendants after you"* (v 7). Circumcision served as the outward, physical sign that a person had made the commitment to follow the laws of God given to the children of the covenant. I can assure you that adult men did not enter into this this decision lightly. A person wouldn't just stand up and say "Yes, I want that," without a firm, heartfelt desire - the prospect of having to go through a circumcision kept out the half-hearted.

There are other verses that add some additional explanations regarding circumcision. First, in regards to importance, circumcision was required. It was to be done as soon as a person wanted to become a Child of the Covenant. Abraham and his 13 year old son, as well as all his male servants, were circumcised on the same day that the covenant was given (17:23). All newborn males were to be circumcised on the 8th day of life. No exceptions were given. If a male descendent of Abraham was not circumcised, he was to be *"cut off from his people"* (17:14). Clearly, obedience to this command, this outward sign of a divine relationship, was vitally important to God.

Second, multiple New Testament verses, like Ephesians 2:11 and Romans 2:28, allude to the "removal of the flesh" aspect of circumcision. The term "flesh" is commonly used to refer to sin or the sinful nature of humanity. In circumcision, "flesh" is physically removed from the body - a visual representation of what is spiritually needed (the removal of sin) to be made clean. Thus, circumcision served not only as a sign of the covenant given to Abraham, but also served as a prophetic representation of what Christ would accomplish for those who would believe in Him.

With this in mind, we read the remarkable statements in Col 2:11 and 12. Baptism is called *"a circumcision made without hands"* and *"the circumcision of Christ."* This circumcision actually removes the *"body of flesh"* (sin), in contrast to the circumcision made *with* hands that only foreshadowed what was to come. This circumcision is infinitely superior to the sign of the covenant given to Abraham, thus making the old sign obsolete. This circumcision is the circumcision of the heart spoken of by Moses (Deu 10:16) and Jeremiah (Jer 4:4). This circumcision allows us to "walk in newness of life" (Rom 6:4).

That baptism removes sin is not a new concept - we saw that in Ephesians 2:38 and Acts 16:16. That baptism connects us to the death and resurrection of Christ is also not new - we read that in Romans 6. What is new is the revelation that baptism is the spiritual circumcision that accomplishes what the physical circumcision could not, the establishment of a relationship with Christ, which enables us to love the Lord with all our heart and soul (Deu 30:6).

9. *1 Peter 3:21: And corresponding to that, baptism now saves you - not by the removal of dirt from the flesh, but by an appeal to God for a clean conscience - through the resurrection of Jesus Christ.*

1 Peter 3:21 is the last verse in Scripture that specifically mentions baptism. It also contains the strongest language linking baptism to salvation: "baptism now saves you". As noted in the Introduction, if this were the only passage someone read from the Bible, there would be no question in their mind about what is needed to obtain salvation. The phrase is clear and succinct. Of course, it isn't the only verse in the Bible, and there are many, many passages which talk about salvation. This verse must be understood in a way that is consistent with the entire scriptural teaching on salvation. It also shouldn't just be dismissed as "confusing" or "misleading."

For those who believe baptism is a "sign," it becomes a bit of a chore to explain Peter's use of this phrase. Their explanation, by necessity, has to traverse various levels and go something like this: "Baptism doesn't really save you. Baptism is a visual representation of what God does for us, wash us clean from sin, by His blood shed on the cross. And faith in Christ as our Lord and Savior is what saves us. So Peter is using that visual picture of baptism to allude to Christ's work on the cross on our behalf. He knows it isn't really baptism that saves us, but he wants to emphasize the necessity of forgiveness for our salvation. In order to make the point in a strong way, he says 'baptism now saves you' which he knows won't be taken literally, rather, readers will understand he means that baptism represents our being justified before God, that is, saved."

Could that explanation be correct? Possibly. Does it fit all the other passages describing baptism? Or is there a better, more straightforward explanation?

If baptism results in the forgiveness of our sins, if it connects us to the body of Christ, if we are linked to Jesus' death and resurrection through baptism, if baptism clothes us in Christ, and if baptism is the circumcision of Christ, made without hands, that allows us to walk in newness of life, then baptism plays an essential role in our salvation. And Peter could say, and mean, *"baptism now saves you."* Not in the sense that baptism alone, apart from faith, saves you. But that baptism, performed as a work of faith, is used by God in a very special way to bring His needed grace into our lives.

Which of these explanations of 1 Peter 3:21 brings unity to these 9 New Testament verses? These are the verses we have to determine the true meaning of baptism. When taken together, do these best give us a picture of baptism as a symbolic "sign," an event meant to remind us of God's goodness, but without any significant relation to salvation; or do they indicate that a vitally important spiritual work occurs in and through baptism - a transformation that is essential in our life as a disciple of Christ?

It has been my observation in the churches I have attended that hold to the "sign" explanation of baptism, that when a baptism occurs, no Scripture is read to introduce or explain what is about to happen. Occasionally Matthew 28:19 is read to indicate that we are commanded to do this thing. Often catechism explanations are offered or illustrations about how

BAPTISM: ITS MEANING

God uses symbols to teach us lessons - but no Scripture. I think the reason is fairly obvious. Scripture tells a different story.

The passages that teach about baptism speak strongly about actual spiritual benefits conferred through baptism. Pastors or ministers would have to spend considerable time explaining why baptism doesn't really mean what the passages are saying. Ironically, these Protestant churches (Orthodox and Catholic Christians fully embrace the aforementioned benefits of baptism) typically pride themselves in being biblically astute and accurate. They hold to the ancient creeds. But when it comes to baptism, they avert their glance. The Nicene Creed clearly states, "I believe in one baptism for the remission of sins." Ask your pastor if he or she believes what is stated in the Nicene Creed. If they say yes, ask if they believe baptism results in the forgiveness of our sin. You may hear them directly contradict themselves in 2 back-to-back answers without the slightest idea that they've done so.

What are the barriers to believing that baptism is so rich in blessings? Why have so many Protestant churches rejected the understanding of baptism that prevailed for the first 15 centuries of the Church?

There are 3 major objections to this understanding which will now be addressed.

Objection 1: Salvation is by faith alone. By saying baptism in any way contributes to our salvation makes salvation a combination of faith plus works, which is heresy.

Answer: Imagine a man who is going to be baptized to please his fiancé. He has been attending church with her and has gone through marital counseling. He doesn't accept that Jesus is the Son of God or any of the teaching about forgiveness or redemption. In fact, he isn't sure if God actually exists. He hasn't revealed this to his fiancé' or anyone else for fear of hurting the relationship. He has been careful to answer all the questions about his beliefs in such a way that everyone thinks he has made a commitment to follow Christ.

Now, this man goes through with the baptism, confessing his (false) faith before a small congregation. He is submersed while the pastor says the words "I baptize you in the name of the Father, and the Son, and the Holy Spirit. Amen."

What just happened? Was a bridge built between God and the man? Were the blessings of forgiveness, adoption into the family of God and connection to the death and resurrection of Christ transferred to this man?

Of course not. The act of baptism without faith is no baptism at all, just a meaningless bath. As is demonstrated in the entirety of Scripture, it is belief in God and trust in the promises of God that brings salvation. The bridge that is built through baptism is built by God, not the pastor or the person being baptized. It is built in response to the faith of the person being baptized. We do not force God to bestow His blessings on us by merely going through the motions of a religious activity, whether it be prayer or confession or baptism. God denounces religious activity done without faith.

Baptism is a work of faith. When the Holy Spirit tells us, *"He that believes and is baptized shall be saved,"* He is not saying belief plus works equals salvation, but rather belief in God plus trust in His promises equals salvation. Going through baptism does not in any way earn for us salvation. Going through baptism with the expectation of receiving God's promised blessings, demonstrates our trust in God.

Those who teach that belief plus baptism amounts to belief plus works, understand faith to be equal to belief - that is, acceptance of certain statements as fact. Faith also includes trust, and trust must be demonstrated.

I may believe that my son can shoot an apple off the top of my head with a crossbow at 50 feet. Really truly believe in my heart that he can do it. But trust dictates that I put an apple on my head, step backwards 50 feet, and have my son aim his crossbow just above my forehead and pull the trigger. Trust is belief put to the test, or faith in action. Seeing baptism as faith in action, brings unity and consistency to all the Scripture that has been thus far presented in this chapter. Trusting that God will do what he has promised through baptism in no way contradicts Paul's words to the Ephesians that *"by grace you have been saved through faith"* (Eph 2:8).

Objection 2: There is too much being attributed to baptism in this explanation. What really matters to God is my heart, not whether I participate in any specific activity.

Answer: This statement is just blatantly false. It is true that God does care deeply about the state of our heart. But He cares equally about our participation in specific activities. This is shown throughout Scripture, from beginning to end. In Gen 6 God asks Abraham to sacrifice his son Isaac. Did God know Abraham's heart? Certainly. Why then did God put Abraham through the agony of preparing his son to be a sacrifice, up to the point of dropping of the knife? Because God requires our faith to be demonstrated. In Gen 16 God commands all 8 day old male infants of Abraham's descendants to have their foreskin removed. If the parents fail to comply, the children are to be "cut off" from God's chosen people. The state of each parent's heart is required to be demonstrated by their actions.

In Leviticus, the priests of Israel were instructed to take a goat, once a year, and to ceremonially place the sins of the nation upon it. It was then released into the wilderness to die. If the nation all believed in their hearts that this was a ridiculous, foolish stunt that accomplished nothing, would God honor that with His forgiveness? Certainly not. Their trust in the promise of God was vital.

What if the priests would have failed to perform the ceremony of the scapegoat? Would God have responded with "Oh well, no matter. I can see the state of their heart and going through with this scapegoat symbolism isn't really necessary?"

No. Israel's trust in, and performance of, this specific activity were both required.

In 2 Kings, Naaman the leper is asked to wash 7 times in the local river to be healed. Elisha could have discerned his heart and merely declared him to be healed. It turns out, that is what Naaman thought he should do (2Ki 5:11). However, it wasn't until Naaman actually went down to the river and bathed 7 times that his leprosy was "washed away" and he was healed. (A foreshadowing of Christian baptism?)

This principle carries through into the New Testament.

During Jesus ministry, he makes it clear that faith demonstrated in action (trust) is not only expected, but brings significant spiritual blessing. When he delivers his famous teaching called the Beatitudes (Matt 5), He declares "Blessed" various groups of people. Five of the 9 blessings are bestowed on people because of their actions: "Blessed are those who mourn, Blessed are the gentle, Blessed are the merciful, Blessed are the peacemakers, Blessed are those who are persecuted for righteousness sake." Jesus did not bless "those who have gentleness in their heart" or " those who have mercy in their heart." No, faith in action is being blessed by God.

BAPTISM: ITS MEANING

Later in His ministry Jesus is teaching his disciples about the cost of following him and he states, *"Everyone who has left houses or brothers or sisters or father or mother or children or farms for My name's sake, will receive many times as much, and will inherit eternal life"* (Mat 16:29).

This abandonment of worldly treasures for the sake of Christ does not earn for us eternal life, rather it demonstrates our trust in Him, an essential component of the faith that leads to salvation.

The Apostle Paul also makes it clear that works of faith are essential. In Rom 10:10 he writes,

"for with the heart a person believes, resulting in righteousness, and with his mouth he confesses, resulting in salvation."

Confessing Christ as Savior is a *work* done in faith. This passage links it to salvation. Should we look at that passage and say Paul is teaching belief (faith) plus works equals salvation? No. As with baptism, confession is not a work that earns anything. Confessing Christ (which can be life threatening) is a demonstration of trust that along with belief constitutes that faith that brings us salvation. The answer to the question of why God uses the act of baptism to bestow so many spiritual gifts on His children belongs to Him alone. Praise be to God for this wonderful provision.

Objection 3: Baptism cannot be required for salvation. It is faith alone that saves. Are you saying that all those who believe but who haven't yet been baptized are not saved?

Answer: In the nine verses that specifically talk about baptism and provide information about its meaning, 2 link it to salvation. Mark 16:16 does so in a way that is clear and precise: *"He that* *believes and is baptized shall be saved."* Note the formula: belief plus demonstration of belief (trust) equals salvation. We saw this just above in Rom 10:10 with a confession of Christ. Yet if Mark 16:16 was the only passage that stated belief and baptism as requirements for salvation, we would need to consider if we were truly interpreting this correctly.

It turns out there are 3 other passages (some would include Heb 10:19-22, making a fourth) that state "water/washing" plus the "word/spirit" are required for salvation.

John 3:5 Jesus answered, "Truly, truly, I say to you, unless one is born of water and the Spirit, he cannot enter into the kingdom of God."

Eph 5:25-27 Husbands love your wives, just as Christ also loved the Church and gave Himself up for her, so that he might sanctify her, having cleansed her by the washing of water with the word, that He might present to Himself the church in all her glory, having no spot or wrinkle or any such thing; but that she would be holy and blameless.

Titus 3:4-6 But when the kindness of God our Savior and His love for mankind appeared, He saved us, not on the basis of deeds which we have done in righteousness, but according to His mercy, by the washing of regeneration and renewing by the Holy Spirit, whom He poured out richly through Jesus Christ our Savior.

Because these verses do not specifically use the word "baptism," some have tried to argue they are not referring to baptism. The question is, how would 1st century listeners understand the phrases "born of water" and "washing of water with the word" and "washing of regeneration?"

BAPTISM: ITS MEANING

These 1st century people were witnessing Jews and non-Jews alike expressing the desire to follow Christ, and then being immediately directed to perform a ceremonial washing in water - baptism. It would be natural and expected that any reference to water or washing used in a spiritual context would be understood as baptism into Christ. What else could these phrases mean?

I have certainly heard some difficult to believe explanations. One is that "born of water" in John 3 means the physical act of being born to our earthly mothers. This would mean Jesus is telling Nicodemus he must be born to his mother and born of the Spirit to be saved. But, He says that being "born again" means being born of the water **and** the Spirit, both.

Explanations that ignore the internal consistency that these verses have with our nine previously considered passages merely cause confusion. John 3:5 reads very much like Mark 16:16. The *"having cleansed her by the washing of water"* phrase of Eph 5:26 is analogous to the washing away of sins stated in Acts 2:38 and Acts 16:22. The *"washing of regeneration"* in Titus 3:5 is spoken of in Rom 6:3,4 as baptism enabling us to *"walk in newness of life."* This understanding makes all these passages internally consistent. And, as we have seen, this understanding does not violate the salvation by grace through faith principle.

What about those who believe that Jesus is the Son of God who died on the cross for their sins, but have not yet been baptized? What is their status?

As we shall see in the next chapter, this was a very rare occurrence. Those who wished to become followers of Jesus were typically baptized on the same day they expressed their desires. The fact that in our present day we have a large number of people who are waiting to be baptized for some reason, whether it be a membership class, or instruction in Christian theology, or attaining a certain age, or waiting for a special date, is frankly unbiblical and attests to the degree that baptism is misunderstood. If you believed that baptism was an essential activity for salvation, and was connected to supernatural blessings, you would feel an urgency to be baptized as quickly as possible.

So, how does God handle this great misunderstanding among those who wait to be baptized? Scripture does not expressly tell us, but there is the principle that God honors the intent of those who seek Him.

Consider the situation where a young man hears the gospel message at a Sunday morning service for the first time and decides he wants to follow Christ. He seeks out the pastor who suggests he be baptized at the evening service. While driving home from church he is involved in a terrible car accident that takes his life. He believes but has not been baptized. Is he saved? Would God honor the intent of this man's heart despite his inability to actually go through with the baptism?

God is not a legalist - one who insists on rule following without consideration for context, contributing factors, and extenuating circumstances. Jesus proved this in his treatment of the thief on the cross. He granted paradise to this man despite the impossibility of baptism. He is not held captive by a 9 word verse in Matthew. God knows the intent of the heart and in this case, it would include being baptized.

By extension, if there is a considerable delay between the onset of belief and baptism due to misunderstanding, inaccurate teaching, pastoral direction, or logistical difficulties, but the intent of the believer is to follow Christ with all their heart, including being baptized, then an unexpected death would not disqualify them from being saved. God sees through time; He is not time bound as we are in this life. Our heart's intent is both blessed and cursed (Mat 5:27,28) as if we had actually completed the action we intend. On the other hand, those who refuse to be baptized, or plan to never be baptized will not be saved. This would fall into the category of not trusting in the promises of God.

Given the tremendous blessings bestowed on the believer through baptism, any delay should be considered foolish. Why would anyone who is passionate about the Gospel of Jesus want to wait to receive forgiveness, the promise of the Spirit, a renewed (circumcised) heart, and adoption into the Body of Christ? Baptism should be the initial, expected response to Christ's invitation to belong to Him. Salvation comes through faith, that is, belief and baptism into Christ.

This explanation of the meaning of baptism brings harmony and unity to all the biblical texts about baptism and its relation to salvation without having to "explain away" or contort the plain meaning of any of the verses.

8

Baptism: Who, When, and How

No issue has divided Protestants more violently and persistently as baptism. The questions of who should be baptized, how they should be baptized, and when it should occur continue to cause divisions. Covenanters tell Lutherans that their baptism as an infant meant nothing, and Presbyterians tell Baptists that being baptized twice is a sin. Meanwhile, Mennonites label the baptism of infants as the "highest and chief abomination of the Pope",[1] despite the fact that ⅔ of the contemporary Christian church (about 1.3 billion persons) support this practice. As with all other questions about Christian doctrine, these need to be answered by considering all the relevant texts we can find that help us pin down the correct answers. This includes all the examples of baptism into Christ found in the New Testament, as well as any other verses with helpful information about who, when, and how.

There are 10 reported examples of Christian baptism given to us in the book of Acts, with an additional baptism mentioned in the book of 1 Corinthians. Of these, 3 are individuals, 3 are households, and the remaining 5 are large group baptisms. Each of these examples will be mined for information. Here is a quick summary of who and where in Scripture they are presented:

1. About 3000 souls at Pentecost - Acts 2
2. Men and women of Samaria - Acts 8:12
3. Simon the Magician - Acts 8:13
4. The Ethiopian Eunuch - Acts 8:38
5. Saul by Ananias - Acts 9:18
6. Cornelius the centurion - Acts 10:47
7. Lydia and her household - Acts 16:15
8. The Jailor and his household - Acts 16:33
9. Many of the Corinthians - Acts 18:8
10. About 12 disciples at Ephesus - Acts 19:5
11. The household of Stephanas - 1 Cor 1:16

We will first answer the question of when, and then how. The question of who should be baptized, with a special focus on the issue of infants and young children, will be presented last given its complex and contentious nature.

When should baptism occur?

If you took a poll of all the pastors, priests, and/or elders in all the churches of all the people reading this book, asking them the question when should an adult attendee at their church undergo baptism, the answers would be strikingly similar, and I would add, strikingly opposed to the biblical examples. The church leaders in every church that I've ever attended would answer this question something like this: "We would first want the adult to go through either a basic Christian doctrine class or membership class so that they can make an informed decision about whether or not they really want to be baptized. We would want to make sure they understand that they are sinners in need of a Savior, that Jesus is God's Son come to earth to live the perfect life that we could not, and that he died on the cross to pay for each of our sins. (Some would add) We would also want the person to understand the commitment they are making to strive to live a Godly life and to be subject to the authority of the church leaders." Many of these leaders would have their pupils consider a set of questions they would ask the person just prior to being baptized. At that point, a date would be set, typically on a Sunday during a church service, on a day convenient for both the person and the pastoral staff. Often this date would be many weeks hence.

Is this consistent with the 11 examples given to us in God's Revelation? In a word, No.

In the 6 examples where the timing of the baptism is specifically given to us, 4 indicate that the people being baptized were baptized *on the same day* that they heard about who Jesus was and what he came to accomplish. The 3000 at Pentecost - the same day they heard the gospel. The Ethiopian on the way to Jerusalem - the same day. The jailor and his household - the same day. Cornelius - the same day. This seems to be more than a biblical suggestion (although less than a mandate).

In the two examples that didn't occur on the same day as the initial gospel message, it did occur as soon as was reasonable. One was the baptism of the Apostle Paul which occurred 3 days after he encountered Jesus on the road to Emmaus. When Ananias, who came to minister to Paul, arrived on the scene, his first directive to Paul was to be baptized.

The other example was a group of about 12 disciples who had not known about the baptism into Christ. As soon as they were informed of its existence, they were baptized (that same day). The other 5 examples do not give us specific timing, although there is no indication that anyone waited to be baptized.

The biblical texts that do indicate timing, convey a sense of urgency. This should not be surprising to us given the importance and significance of baptism.

In the first example of baptism, that of the 3000 at Pentecost, the men are *"pierced to the heart"* after hearing that the crucified Jesus was the promised Messiah. *"What shall we do?"* they ask, desperately trying to figure out how they can make amends to God. Peter's answer is startling:

"Repent, and be baptized each of you for the forgiveness of your sins" (Eph 2:38).

Note he doesn't say, "Repent and go do good works (or penance)." He doesn't say, "Come back tomorrow and hear more of this Jesus." He doesn't say, "I must teach you about all the expectations and glories of being a part of the body of Christ, and then you should be baptized." No. He says repent (turn away from your sinful past) and get baptized. And they did. The text strongly implies they were all baptized on that day. Baptisms were happening fast and furious for multiple hours to get this all done. The Apostles must have felt strongly that this was the important first step in these new disciples' lives.

When Paul was baptized by Ananias, the few words spoken by Ananias that were recorded for us include the admonishment to Paul, *"What are you waiting for"* (Acts 22:16, NIV).

Again, an urgency in his voice. Paul, you shouldn't be sitting there like there is nothing that needs to be done. Get up and get yourself baptized! This was said before any recorded instruction, before any explanation of baptism's meaning, and before any teaching about the Spirit or justification or sanctification. How many churches today say "What are you waiting for?" to their interested attendees on the first day they show up?

In the 2 other specific examples, we find a similar urgency.

When the jailor hears about who Jesus is, he and his household are baptized *"that very hour of the night"* (Acts 16:33).

Really? It couldn't wait until morning? No time to consider the decision? No thought to doing this in the company of all the brethren? Paul does not delay in facilitating this spiritual blessing for this family.

When the Ethiopian hears that there is a baptism into Christ he says to Philip, *"What is preventing me from being baptized"* (Acts 8:36)?

These two men were on a desert road traveling in a chariot. The logical answer from Philip would have been, "Well, we're in the middle of nowhere on the way to Jerusalem. Let's wait until we get to town." Instead, they find water along the way and get it done. Philip demonstrated by his actions the importance he placed on clothing this Ethiopian in Christ.

The timing indicated in these verses is consistent with that recorded in the initial directive to baptize. Matthew 28:19,20:

> *Go therefore and make disciples of all the nations, baptizing them in the name of the Father, and of the Son, and of the Holy Spirit, teaching them to observe all that I commanded you.*

In the making of disciples, baptism should precede the teaching of "all that I commanded you." This ordering is in the Greek text, and is echoed in the examples given to us in Scripture. Baptism should be considered of primary importance in the life of a new believer and should be offered on the same day the desire is expressed. Delaying baptism in no way conforms to the biblical examples, is not consistent with the importance Scripture attributes to it, and should be avoided if possible.

So, how did the church lose this urgency over the past 1500 years? History points to at least 3 reasons.

The first was the mainstreaming of Christianity. In 387, under the rule of Constantine, Christianity became the official religion of Rome, and all Romans were "forced" to become Christian. I put forced in quotes since no one can be forced to believe and trust in Jesus as their Redeemer/Messiah. They can be forced to be baptized, or at least be coerced into being baptized, thus disassociating it from faith, and making it meaningless. When baptism becomes a meaningless ritual, the urgency to partake in the spiritual blessings that come with a real, faith-based baptism is absent. Why be urgent about a ritual that accomplishes nothing?

The second reason the church lost its urgency to perform baptism came with the growth of the 16th century teaching that baptism should be withheld until a person can grasp the full Gospel message and make a confession of their faith. That means understanding what sin is, their own sinfulness, their need of forgiveness, and the provision of Jesus as the perfect sacrifice to atone for their sin. This could take significant time to accomplish, and to assess. By necessity, baptism *had* to lose its urgency in this paradigm. Rushing into baptism would be wrong. Certainly baptizing young children or infants would be inappropriate; these children needed time and instruction before a baptism could be considered. Baptism, understood this way, served as a public confession of faith, a culmination of much thought and consideration regarding the commitment to follow Christ, not the initial step in becoming a disciple.

The third reason baptism lost its urgency came with the understanding of baptism as a "sign" rather than a "bridge," as discussed in the last chapter. Signs are interesting and helpful, but not necessary. A gold ring on a person's left 4th finger tells others something important happened in that person's life, but it is neither necessary, nor does it contribute to actually being married. Taking the ring off doesn't mean anything and waiting to buy one after a wedding is perfectly acceptable. Likewise, if baptism is merely a "sign," a remembrance or acknowledgment of Jesus' redeeming work, then waiting to be baptized is not only acceptable, it may be preferable. Why not wait until a special time in your life, or until a large gathering can be arranged, or until you feel called to be baptized? This may mean many years pass between your initial desire to follow Christ and your actual baptism into Christ. Many in the church do just that.

The problem with these reasons for delay is that they are not supported by scriptural teaching or example. As noted in Matthew 28:16, baptism is meant to be the initial act in making disciples. It is associated with significant and needed spiritual blessings for the person seeking union with Christ. The biblical examples show us that delaying baptism for convenience, or public display, or attaining some level of Christian maturity was unknown in the early church. And as will be demonstrated in the next section on who should be baptized, confession of faith before baptism is not merely uncommon in Scripture, it is the exception to the rule. Baptism is the spiritual gift given to the Church intended to equip, connect, and vitalize every new member of the Body of Christ.

How should baptism be done?

To immerse or not to immerse, that is the question. Some churches have very strong feelings about the answer to this question (typically the immersion group) while others are less concerned about the mechanics and find sprinkling or pouring as valid as immersion.

Baptism is a ceremonial washing. As such, water is required. Could another liquid be used? Scripture speaks only of water (Acts 8:38, Acts 10:47, John 3:5) although the type of water is not specified (ie. river, well, rain).

In the 11 examples of Christian baptism given to us, only 1 gives any sense for how the baptism took place - the baptism of the Ethiopian. The fact that so little is given to us about the "how" would seem to indicate that the method of baptism is not crucial. If it was, the Holy Spirit would surely have communicated this either directly or through multiple examples.

In the one example given to us, Philip is traveling with the Ethiopian on the road from Jerusalem to Gaza.

> Acts 8:36 *As they went along the road, they came to some water; and the eunuch said, "Look! Water! What prevents me from being baptized?"* Verse 38 and 39: *And he ordered the chariot to stop; and they both went down into the water, Philip as well as the eunuch, and he baptized him. When they came up out of the water, the Spirit of the Lord snatched Philip away; and the eunuch no longer saw him, but went on his way rejoicing.*

This passage is one of the three that those who insist on immersion point to to justify their position.

The eunuch went *"down into the water"* to be baptized. Clearly they had come upon a river, pond, or small lake, big enough to go *"down into."* Of course, the problem with using this to support baptism by immersion is that *both* Philip and the eunuch *"went down into the water."* And they both *"came up out of the water."* So unless they both were baptized (clearly not indicated here), the phrase *"went down into the water"* means what you might picture: both men waded into the water, probably to thigh or waist height, to do the baptism.

What happened after that is not given to us. Philip could have laid the eunuch back under the water to do the baptism or he could have used his hands or some other vessel to pour water over the eunuch's head to do the baptism. The text does not give us this detail, nor does it hint at either one. So this one example tells us nothing about the right, or best, way to do a baptism, other than to say using a relatively large, natural body of water for your water source is OK.

The second verse used to justify immersion only is Rom 6:4:

> *Therefore we have been buried with Him through baptism into death, so that as Christ was raised from the dead through the glory of the Father, so we too might walk in newness of life.*

We considered this verse in the last chapter and noted the strong assertion Paul proclaims about baptism - *"we have been buried with Him **through baptism** into death."* Certainly being immersed in water has the appearance of being buried, momentarily, under water. It's understandable that this wording could lead people to conclude that immersion, given its physical appearance, should be, or even must be, the way people are meant to be baptized. But, is this the reason the Spirit of God used these words in this verse? Was this passage written to inform the church about the best method of baptism? Or, is this passage primarily concerned about what baptism does for us? If the latter, then using it as the focal point for supporting immersion only is at best very weak.

In the context of this verse, Paul is reminding the Roman

Christians that their baptism was a transformative event. It linked them with Christ's death *"so that we too might walk in newness of life,"* free from bondage to sin. The context does not support this verse being written to instruct on the best method of baptism. Immersion *may* be the best method, but using Rom 6:4 to decide that immersion is the *only* valid method would be inappropriate. (Beware of constructing controversial Christian doctrine from only 1 verse - especially ones not written for that purpose)

Those are the only 2 passages with some content about the method of Christian baptism. That is very little to go on, given that many in the church have made this such a point of contention.

There is one other passage that is sometimes used to support immersion only, that passage being about the baptism of Jesus. It must be pointed out, however, that Jesus did not undergo a Christian baptism, that is, baptism into the name of the Father, Son, and Holy Spirit. Jesus experienced the baptism of John. That was a baptism of repentance (Luk 3:3), which John was understandably hesitant to perform.

The most detailed narrative is in Matthew 3:

> *Then Jesus arrived from Galilee at the Jordan coming to John, to be baptized by him* (v13). *After being baptized, Jesus came up immediately from the water; and behold, the heavens were opened, and he saw the Spirit of God descending like a dove and lighting on him* (v16).

Proponents of immersion point to the phrase *"came up immediately from the water"* and say that this proves that Jesus was immersed.

The problem with that claim is that the Greek words translated "came up from the water" can alternately be translated "went up out of the water (NIV and KJV)," and "went up from the water (ESV)." The "from" in this verse (Gr, apo) indicates "away from," so that the picture is really Jesus leaving the water rather than Jesus coming up from under the water.

We have all seen beautiful artwork of Jesus standing waist deep in water with the Spirit pictured as a dove descending from above. (How easily we are influenced by non-biblical sources.) The wording in this verse actually indicates that the Spirit came down after Jesus got himself out of (away from) the water.

There is a Greek word for "from under" (Gr, hupokato). If Matthew wanted us to understand that Jesus was under the water and the Spirit came down immediately after Jesus came up from under the water, then that Greek word could have been used to make the passage read "came up immediately from under the water." But, that's not how the Spirit caused this verse to be written.

So, rather than proving that Jesus was immersed, at best this verse conveys that he *could have been* immersed. More specifically, it says nothing about how Jesus was baptized other than that it occurred in the Jordan.

At this point it would be appropriate to ask the question, "Are there any verses that indicate that those baptized were not immersed?"

Of course, there are none that say that a person had water poured over them or that they were sprinkled. That would have ended this conversation long ago. There are, however, examples of baptism that make immersion unlikely.

In the instance of the jailor and his household (Acts 16:33), the passage reads,

BAPTISM: ITS PRACTICE

And he took them the same hour of the night [sometime after midnight] *and washed their wounds; and he was baptized at once, he and all his household.*

This baptism of the jailor and his household occurred in the middle of the night, meaning pitch black outside. It occurred immediately after the jailor washed Paul and Silas' wounds, likely with well water from jugs stored at his house. It is quite hard to imagine that this group of people then all journeyed down to the Krenides River outside the city to find enough water to be immersed, only to come back to the house, all soaking wet, in the blackness of the night, to have the jailor feed them (v 34). People in that time and place typically poured water over themselves to bathe - there were no backyard pools and no running water. It seems much more likely this household baptism occurred in or near the house with water previously stored in jugs or cisterns.

In the account of Paul's baptism (Acts 9), Ananias is led to where he (then Saul) had been staying after his blinding on the road to Damascus. We are told that he is at the house of Judas on the street called Straight. Ananias announces to Saul that he was sent *"so that you may regain your sight and be filled with the Holy Spirit"* (v 17). The passage goes on to state,

And immediately something like scales fell from his eyes, and he regained his sight; then he rose and was baptized; and taking food, he was strengthened. (v18,19)

There is no indication that this series of events, being healed from blindness, rising, being baptized, and taking food, was interrupted by a walk to a lake or river to find a body of water large enough to be immersed. Houses did not come with bathtubs. *"Then he rose and was baptized"* sounds like it was done right then, right there. It is unlikely that Paul was immersed.

In summary, a review of all the passages about Christian baptism in Scripture that could tell us or show us how to conduct a baptism, fails to turn up any evidence that immersion was the commanded or exclusive method. Not one clear example is given. In fact, there is not only no mention of anyone going under water during a baptism, there is good reason to believe that many of the biblical examples occurred in the person's house, not near a source of water big enough for immersion.

There were likely baptisms done by immersion. The revelation that we are *"buried with Christ"* in baptism (Rom 6 and Col 2) may lead some to conclude immersion is the preferred way to be baptized, however, God can certainly accomplish His spiritual work with whatever amount of water we use. Is there any reason to believe that the exact amount of water used to baptize a person or the exact places on the body that the water touches has an effect on the spiritual blessings bestowed by God through baptism? Isn't our faith in God and the promises of God (in this case His promises about what He will accomplish through baptism) what is being blessed, not the details of the water and the body position during baptism?

One last consideration about the method of baptism before moving on. Baptism is a ceremonial washing. This was not a new thing for the children of Abraham. Ceremonial washings for spiritual cleansing date back to the priesthood of Aaron and his sons.

During their initial ceremonial consecration, the Israelites are told to bring Aaron and his sons to the tent of meeting and to *"wash them with water."* (Ex 29:4) This was likely a dousing of water, but clearly not an immersion, since we are told it was done *"at the doorway to the tent of meeting."* Later, in Ex 30,

Aaron and his sons are told to *"wash their hands and feet"* with water from the bronze laver (basin) prior to entering the tent of meeting. They are told to do *this "so that they will not die."*

This was deadly serious ceremonial washing. Part of their bodies were immersed but only a relatively small part of their entire body.

Sprinkling was almost always the method used to apply blood to an object or person, but in Numbers 19 we are told that the sprinkling of water on those who have touched a corpse purifies them from their uncleanness (v13,20).

These verses demonstrates that the 1st century Christians would have been well acquainted with various methods of applying water to a person to receive God's grace.

Who should be baptized?

Before addressing the specific question of who should be baptized, 2 widely held beliefs about baptism need to be dispelled.

The first of these is that baptism is primarily a public confession of faith. As we saw in the last chapter, baptism is primarily something God does for us, not something we do for God. And although we are called to confess God before men (Luk 12:8, Rom 10:9), there is no directive, nor do the examples in Scripture indicate, that baptism needs to be done in a public setting. On the contrary, multiple examples of baptism are done in private. If a public confession was the primary purpose of baptism, Philip would have told the eunuch they should wait until they got to town to perform his baptism. Ananias would have told Saul that they should wait for the next gathering of the brethren for his baptism. Paul would have waited for the next Sabbath to baptize the jailor and his household, rather than doing this in the middle of the night. When Peter baptized Cornelius the centurion and those with him, there is no mention of moving the group to a public place so that others could see this Christian act.

These baptisms show us that a public forum was not considered important. Even in those examples where we are told groups, other than households, were baptized (the 3000 at Pentecost, the 12 disciples at Ephesus), there is no mention of the presence of non-participants to serve as witnesses. The teaching that baptism's main purpose is a public confession is not supported by Scripture and makes baptism something we do for God, diminishing the glory due to God for what He is doing through baptism for us.

The second erroneous belief, related to the first, is that a confession of faith is required prior to being baptized. This is so ingrained in our current practice of baptism that it sounds like heresy to make such a statement. A close examination of the biblical record, however, will prove the point.

In the 11 examples of baptism presented in Scripture, in only one does a confession of faith occur. In Acts 8, in the account of Philip presenting the Gospel to the eunuch on the road to Gaza, we read,

> *As they went along the road, they came to some water; and the eunuch said, "Look! Water! What prevents me from being baptized?" And Philip said, "If you believe with all your heart, you may." And he answered and said, 'I believe that Jesus Christ is the Son of God"* (v36,37).

BAPTISM: ITS PRACTICE

At that point, the chariot is stopped and Philip baptizes the eunuch.

That's it. That's the only example of a confession before baptism. One out of eleven. And it turns out to be a "maybe" one out of eleven.

In most Bibles, if you look at verse 37, you will see either brackets around it or an asterisk marking this verse. The footnote will say something like, "this verse does not appear in the earliest manuscripts."

There are a few other verses like this throughout the New Testament. These verses were likely added by someone making a copy of the original text, which were then propagated by other scribes.

Because these verses are present in most of the copies we now have available to us, they have been left in with this special annotation. So it's unlikely that this one confession even existed in the original letter. But, for sake of argument, let's assume that it's inclusion in Acts was meant by the Spirit. We are still left with the fact that giving a confession before baptism is never mandated, and it's mention in Scripture is as a unique event, rather than the rule. Confessing one's faith in Jesus as Lord became the tradition of the church, very early on, and has persisted to this day. It is a church tradition however, not a biblical requirement.

Given that baptism is not primarily a public confession of faith, and that a confession of faith is not even a requirement, for whom then is baptism meant?

Baptism into Christ, plain and simple, is meant for those who desire to be baptized. This desire needs to be driven by the Spirit's leading after hearing and believing the Gospel - that is, the truth about Jesus being the Son of God, the Messiah, made man for the express purpose of paying for our redemption by His blood on the cross. This is the repeated example given to us in Scripture.

The crowd at Pentecost asks, *"What must we do to be saved?"* Peter states, *"Repent and be baptized,"* and they were. (Note that repentance is not a confession of faith; rather it is an expression of a desire to change one's course)

The Ethiopian eunuch hears the Word, expresses his desire to be baptized, and he is. Cornelius the centurion seeks Peter out, hears the Word, and is baptized, expressing his desire to follow Christ. The jailor, after seeing the faithfulness of Paul and Silas in prison asks, *"Sirs, what must I do to be saved?"* He receives the word of the Lord and *"immediately he was baptized."*

All these people wanted baptism into Christ. It was the natural response to hearing of God's great love for them. There are no stated requirements other than desiring to have your life transformed by the Spirit (i.e. living a life of repentance).

There are stories of well-meaning men through the ages who have understood the importance of baptism and in their zeal for spiritual transformation have forced others to be baptized. One of those men was a General in the Chinese Army.[2] As the history stories tell, he was a convert to Christianity and decided that all the men who fought under him needed to be baptized. Prior to heading into battle, he would line up his troops, and using a large hose, would spray them all down while speaking out the words of baptism, "I baptize you in the name of the Father, and the Son, ..."

Although I don't doubt the faith of this General, performing forced baptisms is nowhere supported by Scripture. Baptism is an act of faith. It is meant for those who have heard the Gospel and desire to follow Christ.

Which brings us to the issue of the baptism of infants and young children.

Two indisputable statements can be made about what Scripture says regarding baptizing the young children of believers:

1. There is no Scripture that says the infants of believers **must** be baptized shortly after birth (unlike circumcision which was mandated on day 8 of life for males born to Jews), and

2. There is no Scripture that says the infants of believers **must not** be baptized shortly after birth.

Thus, any church or person that teaches that *infants must be baptized* or that *infants must not be baptized* are making serious declarations that are not in Scripture. If, in fact, the baptism of infants was of critical spiritual significance, either in performing or not performing, wouldn't the Spirit have included a direct statement in Scripture to guide the Church? A simple "And they were bringing infants to the apostles to have them baptized," or conversely, "Paul instructed the Corinthians to delay baptism for their children until faith matured," would have settled this issue millennia ago. Since no such statements exist, mandates regarding the baptism of infants should not be generated by any Christian group. The question then becomes not one of "must" (or must not) infants be baptized, but one of "should" infants be baptized.

There are certainly directives given in the passages about baptism that could lead one to the conclusion that baptism is not for infants or young children. The instructions to "repent" and "call on the name of the Lord" cannot be done by persons so young.

Many times during this discussion of baptism I have shown that Scripture teaches baptism is for those who have faith; and just above I pointed out that it is for those who desire to follow Christ. Again, young children are not capable of expressing either of these sentiments. But, as it turns out, infants and young children are a special case.

Now, I expect many readers who have grown up in churches that teach that the baptism of infants and young children is not appropriate are thinking, "What? A special case? These youngsters are *not* a special case. Scripture does not say anything about infants being a special case. The passages that instruct us to repent and hear the gospel and believe prior to baptism apply to everyone, thus infants are clearly excluded from the group who should receive baptism."

The irony about that line of thinking is that every Christian church on earth, and I mean every single one, teaches that infants and young children are a special case. Every Christian church teaches that salvation comes by grace through faith in Christ. Yet, infants and young children cannot have faith.[3]

Faith requires knowing who Jesus is, knowing what he came to do, understanding that we are sinners in need of a Savior, and believing and trusting in Him for our righteousness. This is not possible for the very young. If faith in Christ is the criteria for salvation for everyone (no special cases), then all infants and young children who die are doomed to hell.

Thankfully, there is no Christian church on earth that teaches such unbearable doom and gloom. Every church acknowledges that the youngest among us are handled differently by God than those who have developed language, reason, and judgement.

BAPTISM: ITS PRACTICE

Although this realization doesn't answer the question of whether infants should be baptized, it does force the conclusion that God does not hold infants to the same requirements as adults for receiving spiritual blessing, including salvation.

In order to arrive at a reasoned, biblical answer to the question at hand, 2 more fundamental questions have to be answered. First, do infants need the spiritual blessings that come through baptism, and second, would God bestow those blessings on infants who do not yet have faith? If the answer to both of those questions is yes, then arguments for waiting to baptize children fade. If the answer to either (or both) of those questions is no, then clearly, baptism should wait until faith develops.

Most churches that are descendants of the Anabaptist (literally re-baptizers) movement of the mid 1500's teach that infants are a special case when it comes to their need for Christ's redemptive work. All adults are sinners and in need of Christ's forgiveness and justification, but infants and young children are considered "innocent", that is, existing in a state free from condemnation, because they are unable to sin. Sin, in this view, means a willful disobedience of God's commands. Since infants don't have knowledge of God's commands, let alone the ability to generate ethical comparisons in their minds , they are not sinners in need of a Savior. In this paradigm, all infants and young children who die are granted eternal life.

This teaching answers our first question with a "No, infants do not need the spiritual blessings that come through baptism." Baptism, for those Christians who hold to this understanding, is not helpful for infants and should thus be delayed until it is needed.

Does Scripture support the idea that infants are truly "innocents" or does it support the view that infants are not a special case when it comes to needing the redemptive work of Christ?

There are 349 verses in the Old and New Testaments that contain the word "children" or "infants." Reviewing these passages for any that could possibly support the idea that young children are counted as blameless before God, reveals 4 such verses (one of these passages is repeated twice in other Gospels; the three together are counted as one of the four).

The first of these is Matthew 19:13,14:

Then some children were brought to Him so that He might lay His hands on them and pray; and the disciples rebuked them. But Jesus said, "Let the children alone, and do not hinder them from coming to Me. For the kingdom of heaven belongs to such as these."

This same event is recounted in Mark 10:13,14 and Luke 18:15,16. The wording in each of these passages is very similar except that Mark adds that Jesus was "indignant," and Luke starts the account with, "And they were bringing even their babies to Him."

The fact that 3 of the 4 gospel writers were inspired to include this short account of Jesus' encounter with young children attests to its importance for our consideration. Each of these passages reports that Jesus used the phrase, *"For the kingdom of heaven* (or *kingdom of God*, Mark and Luke) *belongs to such as these."*

There are a few possible meanings for this phrase. First, Jesus could have been saying that children are sinless, or blameless, and thus they have a reserved place in heaven. Another meaning could be that the kingdom of heaven belongs to those who are very young, just on the basis of their age (clearly a bizarre take on this phrase). A third explanation is that these children possess a characteristic other than blamelessness that is necessary for a place in God's kingdom.

As is often the case, we must look to other passages to solve this uncertainty. Thankfully, the Spirit anticipated this question and in two of these passages, Mark and Luke, the verse which comes next sheds some light:

Truly I say to you, whoever does not receive the kingdom like a child will not enter it at all. (Mar 10:15, Luk 18:17)

Jesus is telling the adults around Him that the reason the children are being singled out as "owners" of the kingdom is because of how they *"receive the kingdom."* How does a child receive the kingdom? Children, especially if they are young, believe what they are told. They embrace and accept as truth what is presented to them without question. Jesus is teaching the adults that these children belong to the kingdom, not because of some innate goodness, but because they receive the Gospel message without question.

Matthew 18:1-3, the second passage some use to point to children's innocence, reads,

At that time the disciples came to Jesus and said, "Who then is greatest in the kingdom of heaven?" And he called a child unto Himself and set him before them, and said, "Truly I say to you, unless you are converted and become like children, you will not enter the kingdom of heaven."

Once again Jesus is talking to adults, here his disciples, and tells them they need to be like children. Like children how? Certainly this doesn't mean being small or uneducated or physically weak. Could it mean innocent and blameless like children?

No. Telling the disciples that they need to be converted and become sinless to enter God's kingdom would go against the Apostle John's clear teaching that no one is sinless (1Jn 1:8).

The verses just discussed in Mark and Luke are too similar to ignore. They illuminate what "become like children" means. Jesus is telling his disciples they must receive the good news of the Messiah's coming like a child, with full acceptance and trust.

1 Corinthians 14:20 is the third passage which needs to be considered:

Brethren, do not be children in your thinking; yet in evil be infants, but in your thinking be mature.

This verse comes in the middle of an entire chapter dedicated to the right use of the gift of tongues. The Apostle Paul instructs that tongues are be spoken in an orderly fashion, with an interpreter, for the edification of all. He then inserts this verse to encourage maturity. The *"yet in evil be infants"* phrase certainly implies that infants are not evil and he is encouraging his readers to not be evil.

The Greek word for evil used here (Gr, kakia) is used other places to indicate evil deeds and actions (e.g. Col 1:21). Infants are not capable of performing evil deeds and actions. The phrase accomplishes its purpose. It does not however follow from this phrase that infants are blameless or sinless or innocent. That would be adding meaning to the phrase that is just not there.

The fourth verse that some use to support the claim of blameless infants is 1 Cor 7:14. Paul is teaching about how to handle the situation where a believer ends up being married to an unbeliever. Should they divorce? Should they stay married? He states that as long as the unbeliever consents to stay married, they should not divorce. The reason for this is given in verse 14:

> *For the unbelieving husband is sanctified through his wife, and the unbelieving wife is sanctified through her believing husband; otherwise your children would be unclean, but now they are holy.*

A controversial verse to say the least. Adults being "sanctified" through their believing spouse, and the children made "holy." What could this mean?

We can say with certainty that this doesn't mean the unbelieving spouse and the children are automatically saved through a believing parent/spouse. This is made plain in verse 16:

> *For how do you know, O wife, if you will save your husband, and how do you know, O husband, if you will save your wife?"*

Salvation is not guaranteed, but may be facilitated by a believing spouse. By extension, neither are the children automatically saved by a believing parent, but they may facilitate their coming to salvation.

Does "holy" here mean blameless or sinless or innocent? It can't, as it would then also apply to the unbelieving spouse. What does it mean then? In the case of the children, "holy" is juxtaposed against "unclean." Things that are unclean are not able to be presented to God. They must first be made clean, or "holy." Being familially associated with a believer (spouse, parent) does change a person's status before God. Do note that this holiness is a result of the association; the children are not born holy. They are made holy by being the children of a believer.

We see that none of these verses specifically says or could reasonably lead one to the conclusion that humans are born sinless or blameless or innocent. Are there verses that state the opposite - that humans are born sinful or that the very young are not free from condemnation?

There are at least a dozen.[4] The most well-known is likely Psalm 51.5:

> *Behold, I was brought forth in iniquity, and in sin my mother conceived me.*

Most people over the centuries have interpreted this passage as King David lamenting that his sinfulness was a part of him since conception. Those who teach that infants are sinless have had to reinterpret this verse to mean that David is implicating his mother as the sinful one. Yet, this reading makes little sense given its context.

Psalm 51 is David's confession regarding his sinfulness after arranging Bathsheba's husband death in order that he might have her for his wife. Verse 5 is surrounded by David pointing the finger at himself and owning his depth of sin. Verse 2: Wash me thoroughly from *my iniquity* and cleanse me from *my sin*. Verse 3: For I know *my transgressions* and *my sin* is ever before me. Verse 4a: Against You, You only, *I have sinned* and done what is evil in Your sight. Verse 6: *Purify me* with hyssop, and I shall be clean; *Wash me* and I shall be whiter than snow.

David would not interrupt his confession of his own sin by throwing in an accusation about his mother. No, David includes here, in making an account of his life, that he was born in sin, and in fact, sin was present as early as his conception. Obviously this sin was not the sin of rebellious activity. It must be an intrinsic characteristic present in all humans from their beginning.

The Apostle Paul concurs with this assessment. In Romans 3:23 he writes,

For all have sinned and fall short of the glory of God.

The "all" has no exceptions noted. It's not "all except those who are too young to know better." Paul writes this verse after making multiple statements about man's utter sinfulness. *There is none righteous, not even one* (v 10). *There is none who understands, there is none who seeks for God* (v 11). *All have turned aside, together they have become useless; there is none who does good, there is not even one* (v 12).

In case some readers would think that Paul is implicating only those old enough to commit sinful acts, he spends a large portion of chapter 5 discussing how Adam's first sin in the garden resulted in condemnation for all his descendants. Verse 12: *Therefore, just as through one man [Adam] sin entered into the world, and death through sin, and so death spread to all men ...* Verse 15: *For if by the transgression of one the many died ...* Verse 16: *The gift [justification] is not like that which came through the one who sinned; for on the one hand the judgement arose from one transgression resulting in condemnation ...* Verse 17: *For if by the transgression of the one, death reigned through the one ...* Verse 18: *So then as through one transgression there resulted condemnation to all men ...*

Paul repeats over and over the concept that Adam's sin made all his descendants sinful, that is, separated from God. The intimate relationship was broken and that brokenness is passed down to each successive generation. It is part of who we are. It is present in our first hour of life.

Still, a case could be made that all these verses are directed at adults and that children are not held accountable for Adam's actions. Perhaps a more powerful indicator of how God views infants and young children could be gleaned by noting His judgements.

At various times in biblical history, people groups are judged for their wickedness. If infants and young children are viewed by God as sinless and innocent, then His judgements should reflect this and they should be spared any harsh treatments.

This is far from the case. As the Children of Israel are directed by God to do battle with those opposing them, he instructs them to leave no survivors. Men, women *and* children are to be put to death:

> *Deuteronomy 3:1-3 Then we turned and went up the road to Bashan, and Og, king of Bashan, with all his people came out to meet us in battle at Edrei. But the Lord said to me, "Do not fear him for I have delivered him and all his people and his land into your hand. And you shall do to him just as you did to Sihon king of the Amorites* (see Deu 2:31-34), *who lived at Heshbon. So the Lord our God delivered Og also, king of Bashan, with all his people into our hand, and we smote them until no survivor was left.* Verse 6: *We utterly destroyed them, as we did to Sihon, king of Heshbon, utterly destroying the men, women and children of every city.*

In God's judgements, the young are not spared, but suffer the same consequences as their parents.

This judgement upon the very young is not limited to Old Testament battles. In Isaiah 13, the prophet is foretelling the judgement coming in the "Day of the Lord" (v 6). God will command *"My consecrated ones"* to *"execute My anger"* (v 3). He will *"punish the world for its evil and the wicked for their iniquity"* (v 11). He continues,

BAPTISM: ITS PRACTICE

Anyone who is found will be thrust through, and anyone who is captured will fall by the sword. Their little ones will also be dashed to pieces before their eyes." (v 15,16) *And their bows will mow down the young men, they will not even have compassion on the fruit of the womb, nor will their eye pity children.* (v18)

The wrath of God is a fierce and destructive reality.

It is hard for us to picture infants being slaughtered because we like to see them as cuddly and innocent, not worthy of such a horrible end. How could God subject them to such judgement?

The only answer that is consistent with God's character is that these infants are not innocent. They are born into sin, with a heart that opposes God, inheriting the condemnation earned by Adam's first sin. All young children desperately need the grace of God, the righteousness of Christ, just as much as their parents do. In this, they are not a "special case."

Given that infants and young children are sinners in need of a Savior, are the promised blessings granted through baptism available to them without possessing a personal faith?

We've already seen that just being a child of a believing parent makes that child "holy" (1 Cor 7:14). This is not saved, but rather viewed by God differently than if her parents were unbelievers. So, the principle that a child can be spiritually blessed based on a parent's faith appears to be taught in this verse.

Are there other examples?

During Jesus ministry he healed many adults, both spiritually and physically. He often told those who were healed, *"your faith has made you well."* In Luke 8:48, Jesus tells the woman healed of her chronic hemorrhage, *"Daughter, your faith has made you well; go in peace."* Bartimaeus, the blind beggar from Jericho pleads with Jesus to be healed. Jesus says to him (Mark 10:52), *"Go; your faith has made you well."* He was immediately healed. To the lame man brought to Jesus by his friends, He says (after seeing their faith*), "Take courage son; your sins are forgiven."* He follows this up by healing His lameness after the Pharisees challenge His ability to grant this spiritual cleansing (Mat 9:2).

What about when Jesus heals children?

In Luke 8 we read about the death of Jairus' daughter:

> *And there came a man named Jairus, and he was an official of the synagogue; and he fell at Jesus' feet, and began to implore Him to come to his house; for he had an only daughter, about 12 years old, and she was dying* (v 41,42).

On His way to the house, He heals a woman with a chronic hemorrhage. Verse 49 then continues,

> *While he was still speaking, someone came from the house of the synagogue official, saying, "Your daughter has died; do not trouble the Teacher anymore." But when Jesus heard this, He answered him, "Do not be afraid any longer; only believe, and she will be made well."* He entered the house, *took her by the hand, and called saying, 'Child, arise!'" And her spirit returned, and she got up immediately (v 54,55).*

In this instance, the faith that heals Jairus' daughter was *Jairus' faith*! His daughter is brought back from the dead, having her spirit restored, and this had nothing to do with *her* faith. She was dead. The faith of her father *("only believe, and she will be made well"*) is credited for this amazing act of physical healing.

In a similar account, a Canaanite woman pleads for her daughter's spiritual health:

> *And a Canaanite woman from that region came out and began to cry out, "Have mercy on me Lord, Son of David; my daughter is cruelly demon-possessed"* (Mat 15:22).

After a short exchange between Jesus and the woman about her status as a Gentile, Jesus says to her,

> *"O woman, your faith is great; it shall be done for you as you wish." And her daughter was healed at once.* (v 28)

Again we see, more explicitly stated in this account, that the faith of this mother was honored by Jesus and her daughter was spiritually healed. No mention of faith in the daughter, only in her mother.

This principle, that the faith of a parent can result in God bestowing spiritual blessing on a child, without their owning their own faith, includes infants.

When Jesus took infants in His arms and laid hands on them and prayed for them, did He confer significant spiritual benefit upon them (Luke 18:15)? Most certainly. His disciples scolded these mothers telling them to keep the children away. They could not willingly follow Jesus. But Jesus rebuked them and bid the infants come to Him. These infants had no faith, but their mothers did. In faith, they brought their babies to Jesus to be touched and blessed by Him. Isn't this what is happening when a parent brings an infant for baptism? Are they not bringing their infant to be touched (and healed) by Jesus? Should these parents be rebuked?

One last critical observation about the biblical record on baptizing infants before addressing some specific objections.

Imagine you are a Jewish mother (or father) living in Corinth around 50 AD. You are married and have a 3 year old son and a 6 month old daughter. You attend synagogue one Sabbath and hear a man named Paul speak about this Rabbi named Jesus. He opens the Hebrew Scriptures and explains how Jesus is the Messiah, the one prophesied to crush the head of Satan. He is the Son of God come down from heaven in order to be the final sacrifice needed to pay for your sin. You and your spouse's eyes are opened and you believe all this to be true. You, along with others, want to hear more.

On successive Sabbaths Paul teaches that faith in this Jesus is the key to having a right relation with God. He tells those who want to follow this Jesus and be saved that the next step is to be baptized into His name, and to change their lives to live in accordance with the Law of Love. He speaks of this baptism as the circumcision of Christ, done without hands, and that the circumcision done in the flesh, no longer has any merit. You hear from others that in Israel, whole households are baptized together, both men and women. You are also told that the Apostle Peter promised the gift of the Spirit to all those being baptized, and to their children, at Pentecost. You and your spouse step forward with your children to receive this new circumcision - a baptism into the name of the Triune God.

This scenario likely played out thousands of times in the first 2 decades after Jesus' resurrection. Parents would naturally think baptism was also for their children, even their infants, since it was described as a circumcision done by Christ. God commanded the Jews to mark their children at 8 days of age by circumcision, and the Apostles were now saying that the old circumcision of the flesh was obsolete. Would Jewish parents think to themselves, "So, the old circumcision is now of no account. What we need is this new circumcision. This is the first step in belonging to Christ - but it is not meant for our young children."

No Jewish parent would naturally think that, especially since no one was saying it was not for the young children. If the Apostles didn't baptize infants, then each day that baptisms were being performed they would have had to turn away countless young children brought by their parents for baptism: "No, not today." "No, not your young children." "No, not your infants." "No, households don't include infants." "No, your child must be old enough to understand forgiveness." "No, your children should remain "uncircumcised" until they are old enough to confess Christ."

Such a misunderstanding, one that would have caused significant distress, at least among the Jewish community, would have been addressed by one of the New Testament writers. Nearly all of the New Testament books were written after AD 50, yet none say anything about excluding young children from baptism. This silence speaks loudly about the acceptance of adults being baptized **with** their children of all ages.

Objection 1: If baptism links the person baptized with the Body of Christ, then they are saved. Since you can't fall away once a part of the Body, you're saying that infants who are baptized are saved whether they come to faith or not.

Answer: This objection, in large part, drove the Anabaptist movement of the mid 1500's. Many Catholics, at the time, were relying on their baptism as infants as their ticket into heaven, much like the Jews relied on their connection with Abraham. Never mind faith. Never mind living a life of sacrificial love. They had been baptized into Christ and that was enough. They were part of the "I'm saved" club. Those critical of the Catholic Church saw this reliance on baptism as heresy since in the new emphasis, it was faith alone that saved. Baptism was important, but it needed to wait until faith had taken root, and it certainly didn't save anyone. Baptism was meant to show obedience to the command to be baptized and would serve as a public confession of faith.

What was forgotten by those on each end of this spectrum was that salvation requires belief *and* baptism, not one without the other. An infant who does not come to faith, when that faith is possible, or who rejects Jesus as Savior and Lord of their life, severs their relationship with the Body of Christ. Bridges can be broken. Faith, demonstrated in a life of sacrificial love for others, must follow baptism as the evidence that His Spirit is living in their hearts. Also, baptism is not a work we do for God. It is a work God does for us. He promises critical spiritual blessings through participation and does not put an age limitation on who can receive those blessings. The Anabaptist reaction to the idea that salvation can be had through baptism alone, without faith, should have been countered with biblical arguments about the essential nature of faith, rather than declaring infant baptism as worthless and in need of repeat (nowhere taught in Scripture). For their part, Catholics needed to stress that baptism wasn't an irrevocable membership.

Another Protestant group that objects not to infant baptism itself, but to the assertion that baptism links infants with the Body of Christ, are those teaching Reformed theology. This group, which includes Presbyterians, Anglicans, and other reformed denominations, follow the teaching of John Calvin who taught that once a person becomes part of the Body of Christ, they can never be separated from that Body. Unfortunately, this teaching that apostasy (that is, falling away from the Church) does not exist,[5] paints these groups into a corner when it comes to explaining baptism.

The writers of the Westminster Confession, the document expressing the tenets of Reformed theology, were men of character who were striving to be true to Scripture. When explaining baptism, they wanted to convey the importance and spiritual relevance that Scripture gives to it, but could not in any way link it to salvation as this would violate their "once saved, always saved" stance. You can see their struggle in choosing words as they hedge their explanation:

> The efficacy of Baptism is not tied to that moment of time wherein it is administered; yet, notwithstanding, by the right use of this ordinance, the grace promised is not only offered, but really exhibited, and conferred, by the Holy Ghost, to such (whether of age or infants) as that grace belongs unto, according to the counsel of God's own will, in His appointed time. (WC 28.6)

Exactly what the "grace promised" here entails, they do not say. Earlier they say that baptism serves as a "sign and seal" (words Scripture never uses in regards to baptism) of the Covenant of Grace, of in-grafting into Christ, of regeneration, and of the remission of sins (WC 28.1). What does "sign and seal" mean in this context? Again, this is not explained.

So, the words of Scripture are indeed used, along with added words that serve to uncouple the actual blessings of baptism from baptism. The result is confusion about what actually happens during this sacred event. As discussed in the last chapter, baptism accomplishes what the Spirit says it does. Real and essential blessings (not "signs or seals") are conferred without regard for the age of the soul baptized as long as faith underpins the action.

Objection 2: Since there is no specific example of an infant being baptized in the New Testament, I take that to mean infants should not be baptized.

Answer: This turns out to just be a faulty conclusion.

In the New Testament there is no specific example of a women taking Holy Communion, yet all churches welcome women to the Lord's table. In the New Testament there is no specific example of an infant being dedicated, after the resurrection of Jesus, yet nearly all churches that do not baptize infants will perform a dedication. In the New Testament there is not even an example of a confessing teenager being baptized, yet all churches would heartily agree to baptism in this circumstance. The baptism of infants needs to be based on the underlying reasons to do so - their need of Christ's redeeming work and God's demonstrated willingness to confer His grace to the children of believers - not on whether there is a specific example given.

This does, however, bring up the issue of household baptisms. Three times the New Testament reports that a head of household was baptized, along with their "household." Three mentions of anything in the Bible is usually considered an emphasis.

Households in the 1st century tended to be larger than those of the 21st century, often including brothers, in-laws, and grandparents. The term certainly included the children of the head of the household. We are told the Apostle Paul baptized "the household of Stephanus" (1 Cor 1:16), Lydia was baptized "with her household" (Acts 16:15), and the jailor was baptized, "and all his household" (Acts 16:33).

BAPTISM: ITS PRACTICE

Those churches that teach against the baptism of infants explain these verses by saying something like, "Well, there is no certainty that any of these households had any infants, so these verses don't really prove anything."

Although it is true that these households may have been bereft of infants (unlikely since contraception was not readily available), it turns out it doesn't really matter. The Holy Spirit has emphasized the principle that the baptism of households is appropriate, without any stated age exclusion. Additionally, in case one might be inclined to think, "of course very young children would be excluded," we are given the added descriptor in the case of the jailor that he was baptized along with *"all* (Gr, hapas - meaning each and every one) *his household."* So, unless we are comfortable with the idea that the Holy Spirit is purposefully being deceptive by using the word "household" three separate times, we must conclude that Scripture means what is says: baptism of entire households, without age restriction, was common and expected.

Objection 3: If baptizing an infant means they become part of the Body of Christ, then salvation becomes a work of man rather than a work of God.

Answer: When the fathers of the Israelite families in Egypt painted lambs blood on the doorposts of their homes to ward off the Angel of Death, who saved the first-born children - the fathers or God? When Moses led the Children of Israel across the Red Sea to freedom, who saved them - Moses or God? When Joseph took Mary and Jesus to Egypt to escape the slaughter of the innocents, who rescued Jesus from death - Joseph or God? When you (the reader) were brought to faith by the words of your parent or pastor, who saved you - the person bringing you the Gospel or God? In all these examples, salvation came from God *through the specific action of a person.*

This is the usual and common way God brings salvation to His people - by the obedient action of another. The work accomplished in baptism is done by God, but he uses the obedience of the baptizer, just as he has used people from the beginning of biblical history, to be the agent of His grace.

Does this mean that a baptized infant who dies is guaranteed salvation? Scripture never says such a thing, so neither should we. It would, however, be very consistent with the rest of Scripture to expect that God, with His infinite knowledge, would be able to foresee such an infant's coming to faith (or not). Salvation would then be dependent on believing (in this case foreseen by God) and baptism.

What does this mean for an infant of a believer who dies without being baptized? Is this child condemned as one who dies without faith (and baptism)? Again, God is able to see into hearts and into a future to make a perfect judgement. It is likely (though Scripture does not address this specifically) that God honors the intent of the parents in this circumstance.

A final thought to consider: If you ask any Christian parent if they desire forgiveness for their children's sin, if they want their children clothed in Christ, and if they want their children to be members of the Body of Christ, every single one would answer a heartfelt, "Yes!" Ultimately, bringing an infant forward for baptism is a demonstration of faith: trusting that God can and will do what He promises to do through baptism; believing that Jesus is still beckoning infants to come to Him to be touched and healed; and trusting that the promise of the Spirit is indeed for us and for our children. God honors faith.

This explanation of the who, when, and how of baptism brings harmony and unity to all of the Scripture passages that provide information about baptism in a way that is consistent with the foundational principles of Christian teaching.

9

The Lord's Supper

What does it mean to be "present?" Not to be "a present", the noun, or to be "in the present," as in the here and now. Rather, to be present, as in physically in the same place. The controversy surrounding the sacrament of Lord's Supper, celebrated by every Christian Church, hinges on the meaning of this word - present. In what way is Christ present when we take communion, or is He present at all?

The Catholic Church has historically and consistently been at one end of the spectrum on this issue. Transubstantiation is the teaching that after the priest consecrates the bread and wine (declares them sacred), they miraculously become the body and blood of Christ. This is quite a striking claim; one that is difficult for many Christians to accept. It is also itself not wholly clear. Does it become the body and blood of Christ physically? Chemically? What happens to the bread and the wine? Is the presence of the body and blood of Christ a spiritual reality only, not detectable in the physical realm?

The Catechism of the Catholic church explains the presence of Christ in The Lord's Supper in this way:

> Because Christ our Redeemer said that it was truly his body that he was offering under the species of the bread,

it has always been the conviction of the Church of God, and this holy Council now declares again, that by the consecration of the bread and the wine there takes place a change in the whole substance of the bread into the substance of the body of Christ our Lord and of the whole substance of the wine into the substance of his blood. This change the holy Catholic Church has fittingly and properly called transubstantiation.[1]

On the other side of the spectrum is the Southern Baptist church (along with some other Protestant denominations), which teaches that The Lord's Supper is a purely symbolic act meant to commemorate Christ's death. In the words of the church's statement of faith:

The Lord's Supper is a symbolic act of obedience whereby members of the church, through partaking of the bread and the fruit of the vine, memorialize the death of the Redeemer and anticipate His second coming.[2]

There is certainly no talk or suggestion of any real presence of Christ's body and blood in the sacrament.

Between these two viewpoints are a host of explanations as to what extent those who take this Supper are receiving Christ's body and blood. The Lutherans teach, "It is the true body and blood of our Lord Jesus Christ, in and under the bread and the wine which we Christians are commanded by the word of Christ to eat and to drink."[3] This position is quite like the Catholic teaching regarding the real presence of Christ in the sacrament but notes the bread and wine are not transformed into Christ's body and blood, rather they coexist (this position has historically been called consubstantiation). Some Lutheran theologians add that the body and blood of Christ exists supernaturally, not physically as do the bread and wine. Methodist theology acknowledges

Christ's general presence without addressing specifically His body or blood: "In the Lord's Supper, Jesus Christ is present with his worshipping people and gives himself to them as their Lord and Savior. As they eat the bread and drink the wine, through the power of the Holy Spirit they receive Him by faith and with thanksgiving."[4]

The Presbyterians more precisely express the presence of Christ spiritually, but not physically by affirming,

> Worthy receivers, outwardly partaking of the visible elements in this sacrament, do then also inwardly by faith, really and indeed, yet not carnally and corporally, but spiritually, receive, and feed upon Christ crucified, and all benefits of his death: the body and blood of Christ being then, not corporally or carnally, in, with, or under the bread and wine; yet, as really, but spiritually present to the faith of believers in that ordinance, as the elements themselves are to their outward senses.[5]

Translation: Christ's body and blood are truly spiritually present but not in any way physically present in The Lord's Supper.

So, why does any of this matter? Why not let people and churches believe what they will about what is actually going on? Is it hurting anyone if they believe one way or the other? All this confusion - isn't this all semantics? Don't all these teachings boil down to Christ being spiritually present along with the physical signs of the bread and wine?

The problem with this thinking is that some of the above positions could endanger a Christian's faith as well as deter non-Christians who are seeking truth. In particular, the teaching of the Catholic and Orthodox church that the bread and wine truly become, *in substance*, the body and blood of Christ, has serious and important implications. If, in fact, the bread and wine are changed into the true body and blood of Christ after the consecration of the priest, then:

1. Handling dropped crumbs and stray drops is no trivial matter. Likewise, disposing of the unused elements needs to be done in a way that honors the body and blood of Christ - placing in a trash can or dumping down the drain would be unacceptable.
2. The elements would be worthy of worship. As Christ is worthy of worship, so the transformed bread and wine would be worthy recipients of our veneration, admiration, and worship.
3. Partakers must rely on someone to tell them when the bread and wine have been transformed into the body and blood of Christ since this cannot be determined by our senses.
4. During each and every occasion of The Lord's Supper a miraculous transformation occurs. This necessitates calling down the Holy Spirit to perform this miracle.
5. Having the true body and blood of Christ on the altar of the church prior to distribution constitutes offering a sacrifice to God.
6. Those churches that offer The Lord's Supper daily are mimicking the daily presentation of a sacrifice to God as was commanded of the Old Testament priests.
7. Given the complex and profound nature of this Supper, only trained priests should ever offer this sacrament.
8. By definition, partakers of The Lord's Supper are participating in a type of cannibalism since they are ingesting the body and blood of Jesus who is fully human in addition to being fully God.

Both the Catholic and Orthodox churches acknowledge and embrace all of the above implications except for number 8. The notion of cannibalism is generally aberrant to all people, so despite the obvious connection to eating human flesh and blood, this implication is denied.

Most Protestants find all 8 implications of eating the real flesh and blood of Christ troubling. Most concerning may be the language describing The Lord's Supper as a sacrifice. In biblical usage, sacrifices are offered to God as a means to gain forgiveness for sin. Jesus' death was the final sacrifice as attested to in Hebrews:

> *For it was fitting for us to have such a high priest, holy, innocent, undefiled, separated from sinners and exalted above the heavens; who does not need daily, like those high priests, to offer up sacrifices, first for His own sins and then for the sins of the people, because this He did once for all when He offered up Himself. (Heb 7:26,27)*

Scripture must dictate our belief regarding all aspects of this sacrament, so it is time to gather up all the pertinent biblical passages and work through their meaning in a way that is reasonable and consistent with all other Scripture. There are 7 such passages:

1. Matthew 26:26-28
2. Mark 14:22-24
3. Luke 22:19-20
4. John 6:30-59
5. 1 Cor 10:16-21
6. 1 Cor 11:23-26
7. 1 Cor 11:27-34

THE LORD'S SUPPER

The Matthew, Mark, Luke, and 1 Cor 11:23-26 passages are quite similar and give an account of what Jesus said and did during that Last Supper. As a representative sample we will look at the 1 Corinthians verse noting any differences from the others.

For I received from the Lord that which I also delivered to you, that the Lord Jesus in the night in which He was betrayed, took bread, and when he had given thanks He broke it and said, "This is My body which is for you; do this in remembrance of Me." In the same way He took the cup after supper, saying, "This cup is the new covenant in My blood; do this as often as you drink it in remembrance of me." For as often as you eat this bread and drink the cup, you proclaim the Lord's death until He comes. 1 Cor 11:23-26

Question: Did Jesus ever speak in metaphors? In all four accounts, Jesus is holding a broken loaf of bread in His hands and says, "This is my body." The disciples are all looking at the loaf, trying to make sense of what He is saying. He is God. He could certainly make the loaf into the same substance as His body should He choose to. The words He speaks are quite plain. Or, this could be a metaphor, meaning that the bread in His hands is meant to represent His body. If that is the case, he is saying, "this bread *is* My body" to emphasize His point - the point being that He is the bread of Life, required for spiritual nourishment for all who desire eternal life.

During His ministry, Jesus used parables extensively to teach about the Kingdom and about God. Parables are by definition not literal. They are often introduced using similes - this thing I am trying to teach you about *is like* this other thing that you can picture and know about. "The kingdom of heaven *is like* a mustard seed" (Mat 13:31). "The kingdom of heaven *is like* leaven" (Mat 13:33). "The kingdom of heaven *is like* a treasure hidden in a field" (Mat 13:44). "The kingdom of heaven *is like* a landowner" (Mat 20:1). "The kingdom of God *is like* a man who casts seed upon the soil" (Mark 4:26).

What about metaphors? Did Jesus ever use metaphors? Yes, many times. Jesus said, "I am the bread that came down from heaven" (Jn 6:41); "I am the light of the world" (Jn 8:12); "I am the door" (Jn 10:9); "I am the good shepherd" (Jn 10:14); "I am the vine" (John 15:5). Jesus is clearly not bread or a light or a door or a shepherd or a vine. But, as was His mode of teaching, He called Himself these common objects to give us a better picture of what He is like and what He came to do.

In all 4 accounts of what happened during Jesus' last supper with His disciples, it is recorded that He holds up a loaf of bread, gives thanks, and says, "This is my body." This could certainly be a kind of reverse metaphor - not I am (like) this common thing, but this common thing is (like) my body. There is no evidence in these verses that the disciples thought they were eating the actual flesh of Jesus or that any transformation took place to change the substance of the bread into Jesus' body. No apostolic questioning of "How could this be?" or prayers for a miracle. The use of a metaphor here by Jesus would be very consistent with His many other teachings directed toward the 12 apostles.

"Do this in remembrance of me." This instruction occurs in 2 of the 4 accounts and gives us our first explanation of what the purpose of this special meal was - a remembrance of Jesus. What specifically are we to remember about Jesus? The broken bread and the cup of wine are to call to mind the great sacrifice He provided on our behalf. This is further explained in the last sentence of this passage: "For as often as you eat this bread and drink the cup, you proclaim the Lord's death until He comes." A remembrance and a proclamation of the death of Christ. Note

also that Jesus identifies what they just ate as "bread", not His "body." This supports the interpretation that Jesus was using a metaphor when He previously spoke "This is My body," or at least was confirming that the bread was still bread, not something else.

"This cup is the new covenant in My blood." Although we tend to think Jesus said "This is My body," and "This is My blood," to the apostles, He did not. Matthew and Mark record that Jesus said, "This is My blood of the covenant," while Luke and the 1 Corinthians passage record, "This cup is the new covenant in My blood." Why the difference and why did He deviate from the expected "This is My blood" to echo "This is My body?" Jesus clearly wants to emphasize that a new covenant, or promise, is being created between God and man. No longer must His people rely on the priests to offer endless sacrifices to atone for their sins. The Messiah had come to lay down His life for His people as a final sacrifice. Obedience to the law would no longer be the measure of their relationship to God, rather faith in His Son as their Redeemer would be the single requirement.

As far as the difference in the two accounts is concerned, apparently these two phrases were considered to be equivalent by the apostles and the Holy Spirit. It is not likely He said them both. Note the more obvious metaphor here: *"This cup is the new covenant..."* The cup was not a written or spoken promise; it was a cup with wine in it. The cup, and its contents, represented the death of Christ and the beginning of a new era. Jesus could have given the apostles these instructions after He had risen or via the Spirit after His ascension into heaven. Instead He stood before them, flesh and blood intact, and said, *"This is My body,"* and *"This cup is the new covenant in My blood."* The apostles would not have taken these words to mean that Jesus had transformed the bread into the same substance as

His body and the wine into the same substance as His blood.

After Jesus is finished passing the bread and the wine, Matthew and Mark tell us that He says to them, *"Truly I say to you, I will never again drink of the fruit of the vine until that day that I drink it new in the kingdom of God."* He wants to impress upon them that this is it. He had been traveling and teaching and eating with them for a few years, but this was truly their last supper. He was leaving them. We must also note that Jesus identifies what the apostles just drank as *"the fruit of the vine."* He also speaks of it as something He has drunk before and something He will drink again. It really makes no sense to suppose that He is talking about drinking His own body and blood.

To summarize these 4 passages, it would be reasonable to say that Jesus is instructing His followers that when they gather together for worship, they should take some bread and some wine, give thanks to God for His provision of Christ as the perfect sacrifice for their sin, and then eat and drink, solemnly remembering His crucifixion on our behalf. Nothing more can really be gleaned or inferred from these texts. There is no convincing argument that Jesus is telling us that the bread and wine are changed into His true body and blood, or even that His body and blood are present in the elements beyond a remembrance in our mind.

The Holy Spirit has given us 3 other passages to consider that are vitally important to our full understanding. The first of these is the continuation of the 1 Cor 11 verses discussed above. Starting at verse 27, Paul says,

> *Therefore,* [that is since taking The Lord's Supper is proclaiming the Lord's death, v 26], *whoever eats the bread and drinks the cup of the Lord in an unworthy*

manner, shall be guilty of the body and blood of our Lord.

What *might "in an unworthy manner"* mean, and what about *"shall be guilty of the body and blood of our Lord?"* To answer the first, we need to look back in chapter 11, just before Paul's recounting of Christ's instructions to His disciples. Paul is retelling the story of Christ's last supper, mid-chapter, as part of a chastising of the Corinthians for making light of this Supper by either arriving hungry and using it as a meal to fill their stomachs, or overindulging in the wine and becoming drunk. He says in verse 20 and 21, *"Therefore when you meet together, it is not to eat the Lord's Supper, for in your eating each one takes his own supper first; and one is hungry and the other is drunk."*

He goes on to express his disgust in no uncertain terms:

"What! Do you not have houses in which to eat and drink? Or do you despise the church of God and shame those who have nothing? What shall I say to you? Should I praise you? In this I will not praise you" (v 22).

These people were partaking of the Sacrament in an unworthy manner by not regarding it as holy and sacred. Rather, it was just a chance to get some food and wine. But Paul adds a twist to this indictment by saying that those who do this are *"guilty of the body and blood of our Lord."* He could have left this out. Or he could have said something like "in so doing, you dishonor the symbols of Christ's body and blood." Is this merely some additional metaphorical phrasing? It appears not. In verse 28 Paul continues, *"But a man must examine himself, and in so doing he is to eat of the bread and drink of the cup."* (Again affirming it is bread and wine that is being consumed) *"For he who eats and drinks, eats and drinks judgement to himself if he does not judge the body rightly."*

It should come as no surprise that the Christian Church has struggled over the years with describing what is taking place during this celebration. Both Jesus and Paul seem to use the terms bread and body interchangeably as well as wine and blood. One the one hand, they both make clear that what is being eaten is bread and drank is wine. On the other hand, people are being judged *"guilty of the body and blood of Christ"* for not partaking of The Supper rightly. The judgement has been physical illness and occasionally death (v 30)! This is no trivial matter. We need some more information.

Turning to 1 Cor 10, Paul is warning the Corinthians to not be like the world. Such behaviors lead to destruction. He specifically cites idolatry (v 7), sexual immorality (v 8), grumbling (v 10), and tempting Christ (v 9). He further warns against participating in demonic rituals by contrasting this with taking the bread and cup: *"Is not the cup of blessing which we bless a sharing in the blood of Christ? Is not the bread that we break a sharing in the body of Christ"* (v 16)? These are rhetorical questions with the clear answer, Yes. The Greek word used for "sharing in," koinonia, is translated "communion of" in the King James, and "participation in" in the English Standard version.

Koinonia always has the sense of bringing things together into a close relationship. It is most often translated as "fellowship" as in 1 John 1:3: *"What we have seen and heard we proclaim unto you also, so that you too may have fellowship (koinonia) with us; and indeed our fellowship (koinonia) is with the Father and with His Son, Jesus Christ."* And 1 Cor 1:9, *"God is faithful, through whom you were called into fellowship (koinonia) with His Son, Jesus Christ our Lord."*

The bread and the body of Christ are in a koinonia relationship - brought together in fellowship. The wine and the blood of Christ are in a koinonia relationship - brought together in fellowship. The bread still exists, as does the wine. But the body and blood of Christ are also there. Somehow. We are not told how, any more than we are told how Jesus is fully God and fully human. For those who teach the bread and wine are symbols only and that God's body and blood are not present, are not in "koinonia" with the bread and the wine, they miss a glorious reality. They fail to *"judge the body rightly."* Looking back at Jesus' words, *"This is my body,"* we can now see that this was not a true metaphor. Jesus was saying, Yes, this is bread, but it is also my body. The two are present at the same time.

This explanation brings harmony to all the verses we have considered so far. It is consistent and in no way contradicts any of the phrases or meanings given to us. However, it once again raises the question about whether the Lord's Supper is a sacrifice. If the body and blood of Christ are present with the bread and the wine, in what way are they present? If physically present, then the implications listed at the beginning of this chapter hold true.

The 1 Corinthian 10 verses continue with the only use of the word "sacrifice" in proximity to teaching about the bread and the wine. Paul contrasts those who "drink of the cup of the Lord" and those who drink "the cup of demons" (v 21). He does not wish any who are part of the Body of Christ to participate in any way with those who are given over to worshipping the demonic. He warns,

> Look at the nation Israel; are not those who eat the sacrifices sharers in the altar? What do I mean then? That a thing sacrificed to idols is anything, or that an idol is anything? No, but I say that the things which the Gentiles sacrifice, they sacrifice to demons and not to

God; and I do not want you to become sharers in demons (vv 18-20).

He continues with instruction about the eating of food sacrificed to idols. Apparently, there was some controversy about whether a Christian could in good conscience eat any food that was once on an altar being sacrificed to an idol. He says for conscience' sake, a Christian should not eat any such food if he is specifically told it once sat on a idol's altar - not because it would violate the Christian's conscience, but for the sake of the one who made the effort to point it out:

But if anyone says to you, 'This is meat sacrificed to idols,' do not eat it, for the sake of the one who informed you, and for conscience' sake; I mean not your own conscience, but the other man's; for why is my freedom judged by another's conscience (vv 28,29)?

So, is Paul here equating the sacrifice made to idols to the Lord's Supper? That is, does he see both as a sacrifice? He clearly sees the Lord's Supper as something that links us to Christ and to one another: *"Since there is one bread, we who are many are one body; for we all partake of the one bread"* (v 17). He also sees those who sacrifice to demons as partakers of the demonic. But, he never says anything like "the sacrifice of the bread and wine," or "the sacrifice of the Lord's altar." The two are contrasted but never compared.

Paul summarizes the point of this illustration in the middle of this section of Scripture by stating, *"All things are lawful, but not all things are profitable. All things are lawful, but not all things edify. Let no one seek his own good, but that of his neighbor"* (vv 23,24). Paul is not trying to teach us that the Lord's Supper is a sacrifice. He is using the sacrifices offered by the ungodly to teach us how to approach their behaviors. We are not to participate in any way that could be misinterpreted or would lead them to think what they are doing is OK. How they handle God's creation does not poison it or somehow curse it. We should always behave in such a way that by our actions we *"give no offense"* (v 32) and seek others benefit *"so that they may be saved"* (v 33).

Teaching that the Lord's Supper involves a recurring sacrifice of the body and blood of Christ, or using the words of the Catholic Catechism, that the Eucharistic sacrifice "re-presents the sacrifice of the cross[6]," is confusing and damaging to the Gospel. The Gospel message is that Jesus left His heavenly realm, became fully human, lived a holy life and died on our behalf, as the final and all sufficient sacrifice, to redeem us from destruction. To talk about, or witness, the daily presenting of the body and blood of Christ as a sacrifice, to Christ, calls into question whether Christ's work on the cross did what Scripture says it did. The writer of Hebrews emphasizes that Christ's sacrifice was a singular event, efficacious once for all. Besides Heb 7:26,27 (see above), He states,

> *nor was it that He [Christ] would offer himself often, as the high priest enters the holy place year by year to offer blood not his own. Otherwise He would have needed to suffer often since the foundation of the world; but now once at the consummation of the ages He has been manifested to put away sin by the sacrifice of Himself (Heb 9:25,26).*

And again in Heb 10:12: *"but He [Christ], having offered one sacrifice for sins for all time, sat down at the right hand of God."*

The Lord's Supper is a beautiful memorial to His glorious sacrifice, but it is not a sacrifice.

Christ's presence in the bread and wine, should one want a description of how they are present, would best be described as spiritual. Scripture does not use this word, so those who choose to describe His presence as "a mystery" (as the Orthodox do) are merely reflecting what Scripture gives to us - we are not given a clear explanation of how His body and blood exist in "koinonia" with the bread and wine. Yet, as bread and wine are food for the body, Christ's body and blood, spiritually present, would certainly be food for our souls. This feeding of our souls would not occur in any physical way but would be present at the spiritual level. Paul attests to the fact our spirits can feed on Christ in 1 Corinthians:

all ate the same spiritual food; and all drank the same spiritual drink, for they were drinking from a spiritual rock which followed them; and the rock was Christ. (10:3,4)

To add the adjective "real" to describe Christ's presence should not be necessary. His presence is not a fake presence. It's likely those who want to insert the word "real" want to make the point that He is not just present in our memories, or symbolically. Indeed, as noted above, Christ's body and blood are truly present and we must not water down this significance as some in the Corinthian church did.

The last passage for consideration might be the most important as it could provide the best argument for transubstantiation. John chapter 6 contains what many call Jesus' Bread of Life Discourse. It occurs just after Jesus feeds about 5000 people with five barley loaves of bread and two fish, and after He walks on water on the sea of Galilee. Jesus is teaching in the synagogue in Capernaum the next day when He answers the crowd's call for Him to give them a sign such as the provision of manna from heaven. He says,

THE LORD'S SUPPER

> *Truly, truly, I say to you, it is not Moses who has given you the bread out of heaven, but it is My Father who gives you the true bread out of heaven. For the bread of God is that which comes down out of heaven, and gives life to the world." Then they said to Him, "Lord, always give us this bread." Jesus said to them, "I am the bread of life; he who comes to Me will not hunger, and he who believes in Me will never thirst" (vv 32-35).*

Jesus' self-identification as *"the bread of life"* here echoes some of His other descriptors for Himself. He states He is *"the light of the world"* in John 8:12. In John 15:5 He declares, *"I am the vine, you are the branches."* The book of John records many of Jesus' teachings where He uses picture language (in this case metaphors) to drive home His divine characteristics. Just as bread was essential to physical life for the 1st century Jews, so Jesus is essential for their eternal life. Just as a vine provides all the nourishment for branches to live, so Jesus provides all that we need to live eternally.

Jesus then goes on to say, four times in four separate verses, that His followers must eat His flesh and drink His blood. Starting at verse 53,

> *So Jesus said to them, 'Truly, truly, I say to you, unless you eat the flesh of the Son of Man and drink His blood, you have no life in yourselves. He who eats My flesh and drinks My blood has eternal life, and I will raise him up on the last day. For My flesh is true food and My blood is true drink. He who eats My flesh and drinks My blood abides in Me and I in him. As the living Father sent Me, and I live because of the Father, so he who eats Me, he also will live because of Me. (vv 53-57)*

It is only natural listening to Jesus speak of His followers eating His flesh and blood to think of the Lord's Supper. In fact, most of the early Church leaders considered this as a foreshadowing of the instructions Jesus gave to His disciples in the upper room just before He was betrayed. The words were clearly taken literally by many who heard Him speak. In response, they asked, *"How can this man give us His flesh to eat"* (v 52)? Many of His followers turned away from Him at this point, unable to accept that they must eat His flesh and blood (v 66). They said, *"This is a difficult statement, who can listen to it?"*

If Jesus was talking about His follower's participation in the Lord's Supper in these verses, then those who teach transubstantiation have here a substantial piece of evidence. Doesn't Jesus say, *"My flesh is true food, and My blood is true drink"* (v 55)? Doesn't He say, *"I am the living bread that came down out of heaven; if anyone eats of this bread, he will live forever; and the bread also which I will give for the life of the world is My flesh"* (v 51)? These verses would support a true change of the bread into Christ's body and the wine into Christ's blood, if He is talking about our taking of the Lord's Supper. But, as always, if this is the right interpretation, then it must also be consistent with the rest of Scripture.

Considering these verses more closely, one can see a huge problem with thinking Jesus is talking about the Lord's Supper here. Note the requirement for salvation that Jesus says is linked to this eating and drinking of His body and blood: *"He who eats My flesh and drinks My blood has eternal life, and I will raise him up on the last day"* (v 54). He states it more emphatically in the prior verse: *"Truly, truly I say to you, **unless** you eat the flesh of the Son of Man and drink His blood, you have no life in yourselves"* (v 53). He repeats it again in verse 57, *"As the living Father sent Me, so I live because of the Father, so he who eats Me, he also will live because of Me."*

Is taking the Lord's Supper required for salvation? Is taking the Lord's Supper required to be a disciple of Christ? In no other place in Scripture is this stated or implied. No church (including the Catholic church) teaches this. When Jesus instituted the Lord's Supper, He stated *"Do this in remembrance of Me."* He gave them no hint that taking this sacred meal was required for their redemption. There are no words in all of Scripture linking this meal to justification or salvation. Surely, if this were the case, He would have told them in no uncertain terms at the time He gave them this spiritual blessing.

Another way to understand Jesus' words about eating and drinking His flesh and blood, and one that would be complementary to the rest of John 6, is in the sense of fully and completely participating in Christ. The phrase *"to drink the cup"* can mean to experience something fully, rather than just watch as a bystander. Jesus uses this when talking to His disciples about His impending death. He asks them, *"Are you able to drink the cup that I am about to drink?" They said to Him, "We are able"* (Mat 20:22).

Jesus was not asking them about swallowing some liquid. He was challenging them to see that only He could be the required sacrifice for our sin. (They failed to comprehend) In the last half of John 6, Jesus tries to make the point that believing in Him does not mean merely possessing knowledge of who He is (as the demons did). Believing in Him means relying and trusting on Him for our daily sustenance. It means taking Him into our inmost being. It means dying to our fleshly desires and taking up our cross, just as He did, with the Spirit's help. This type of eating and drinking of Christ's body and blood is necessary for salvation.

When Jesus physically left this earth to join His Father in Heaven, He left us a gift. This unusual gift simultaneously feeds our souls, reminds us of His Divine love for us, and proclaims His death to all the world. He offers this gift to us whenever we assemble to worship His majesty. Praise be to God for His provision.

The most common objection I have heard to this explanation of the Lord's Supper goes something like this:

Objection: All this talk of picture language and metaphors is dangerous. Shouldn't we be taking the Bible as literally as possible? Haven't certain people taught that Jesus is really a metaphor - that He didn't really exist but stands for living a sacrificial life. Couldn't the whole Bible be taken as a metaphor about being a good person? Where does it end?

Answer: This is a fair and important question. The determination about what language should be taken literally and what should be taken as symbolic or representative can be challenging. Are the 1000 years in Revelation 20 a literal 1000 earth years or something else? Is the story of Noah's ark literal or merely a parable, a warning of God's displeasure with sin? When Jesus said, *"If your right eye makes you stumble, tear it out and throw it from you"* (Mat 5:29), was He expecting His followers to take this literally and actually carry this out? When Jesus said, *"unless one is born again he cannot see the kingdom of God"* (John 3:3), was he speaking literally or figuratively? Most Christians would probably answer those 4 questions, "Not sure, literal, figurative, literal," with the caveat that the "born" in "born again" in John 3 means something different than the usual usage of the word.

So, how do we know? How do we judge wisely when determining the right meaning of a phrase?

The first step is to acknowledge that a passage could have more than 1 meaning. Some have many possible meanings. To rigidly hold to one meaning, whether literal or not, without considering the possibilities is to put blinders on. Blinders make sure a specific path is taken; problem is, it may be the wrong path. The second step is to realize that Jesus' preferred method of teaching was through parables - fictional stories designed to teach an underlying truth. Matthew tells us, *"All these things Jesus spoke to the crowds in parables, and He did not speak to them without a parable"* (Mat 13:34). Sometimes these stories are identified as such: *"Hear then the parable of the sower"* (Mat 13:18). Other times they are not, such as the story of the prodigal son, *"And He said, A man had two sons..."* (Luk 15:11). Because this story is told in the midst of other parables, no one doubts that this too was a fictional story told to teach a lesson.

When it comes to phrases such as *"baptism now saves you,"* and *"you must be born again,"* and *"this is my body,"* great care must be taken to not only consider multiple possible meanings, but to assure any meaning assigned to the phrase is consistent with all other Scripture - the third step. As we saw in the above arguments, to assign the meaning "the bread is turned into Christ's body" to the phrase *"this is my body"* is not consistent with all the passages that identify what is being eaten as "bread." On the other hand, the meaning "this bread represents my body (only)" is also not consistent with the passages that speak of the union of Christ's body and blood with the bread and wine. Neither of these fit. What fits is something in-between.

There will always be discussion and thoughtful insights into the nuances of biblical texts. Not everything will be made clear to our limited human reason. But, two mutually exclusive views cannot both be right, and interpretations that damage or diminish the work of Jesus Christ must be confronted.

10

Prayer, Confession, and Forgiveness

Hail Mary, full of grace, the Lord is with thee; blessed art thou among women, and blessed is the fruit of thy womb, Jesus. Holy Mary, Mother of God, pray for us sinners, now and at the hour of our death. Amen.

Prayer

This prayer to Mary, the mother of Jesus, is known by heart and recited by 100's of millions of Christians worldwide each week. Catholics find comfort in reciting this prayer, while Protestants find it troubling. Is praying to Mary, or any other human for that matter, OK? Do they hear our prayers? Are they in a position to act on our prayers? Does God encourage this type of prayer?

Prayer has been the expected mode of communication between God and His people from the earliest of times. From the fourth chapter of Genesis, where we are told *"men began to call upon the name of the Lord"* (v 26), to the 3rd Book of John in the New Testament where the Apostle tell Gaius, *"I pray that in all aspects you may prosper and be in good health"* (1:2), those seeking God are engaged in prayer. The Apostle Paul tells us to *"pray without ceasing"* (1Th 5:17). We are told that Jesus often slipped away from the crowds to pray in the wilderness (Luk 5:16). He spent the last hours before His betrayal praying to His Father (Mat 26:36-44), and on the cross His last words are a confident prayer of trust: *"Father, into your hands I commit my Spirit"* (Luk 23:46).

Most of us should be praying much more than we currently do. But what exactly should we be praying about? And to whom should we be praying?

There are books upon books written about prayer. Some are written for instruction, some for encouragement. Some describe mystical experiences obtained through prayer, while others suggest prayer can be a simple attitude of thanksgiving and dependence as we go about our daily duties.

Jesus gave some specific instruction in His famous teaching about prayer during His sermon on the mount. In Matthew 6 He says,

> *Pray then in this way, "Our Father, who is in heaven, hallowed be thy name. Your kingdom come, your will be done on earth as it is in heaven. Give us this day our daily bread. And forgive us our debts, as we also have forgiven our debtors. And do not lead us into temptation, but deliver us from evil" (v 9-13).*

Most Christians know this as the Lord's Prayer and are taught to pray this from a young age. Most churches pray this prayer corporately at some time during each month.

This teaching about prayer is echoed in the book of Luke. In chapter 11, in response to a request by one of the disciples, *"Teach us to pray,"* Jesus repeats this basic framework: address God as "Father"; acknowledge His position in heaven and His right to be revered; express a desire for His will to be done; ask for our daily needs to be met; ask for forgiveness; lastly, ask for protection and rescue from evil. Any prayer offered by a child of God containing these basic elements should be appropriate and pleasing to God.

What else does Scripture tell us about content? There are over 200 verses in both the Old and New Testaments that directly mention prayer or praying, so a complete rundown is not possible here. Fifteen representative verses that give content related information will be briefly summarized.

Gen 32:11 - *Deliver me, I pray, from the hand of my brother, from the hand of Esau; for I fear him that he will come and attack me and the mothers with the children.* A prayer for physical protection from a threat.

Ex 33:13 - *Now therefore, I pray You, if I have found favor in your sight, let me know your ways, that I might know You, so that I may find favor in your sight.* A prayer for a better understanding of God.

Num 12:13 - *Moses cried out to the Lord, saying, "O God, heal her, I pray!"* A prayer for another's healing [in this case, the leprosy of Miriam].

Num 14:17 - *But now, I pray, let the power of the Lord be great, just as You have declared.* A prayer for God to demonstrate His power.

1 Sam 23:11 - *Will the men of Keilah surrender me into his hand? Will Saul come down just as your servant has heard? O Lord God of Israel, I pray, tell your servant. And the Lord said, "He will come down."* A prayer for specific knowledge regarding those who seek your harm.

PRAYER, CONFESSION, FORGIVENESS

2 Ki 6:18 - *When they came down to him, Elisha prayed to the Lord and said, "Strike this people with blindness, I pray." So He struck them with blindness according to the word of Elisha.* A prayer to hinder the enemies of God.

2 Ch 6:40 - *Now, O my God, I pray, let Your eyes be open and Your ears attentive to the prayers offered in this place.* A prayer for God's attention.

Jer 29:7 - *Seek the welfare of the city where I have sent you into exile, and pray to the Lord on its behalf; for in its welfare, you will have welfare.* A prayer for the prospering of a people group.

Mar 14:35 - *And He went a little beyond them, and fell to the ground and began to pray that if it were possible, the hour might pass Him by.* A prayer for relief of suffering.

2 Cor 13:7 - *Now we pray to God that you do no wrong.* A prayer for another's behaviors.

2 Cor 13:9 - *For we rejoice when we ourselves are weak, but you are strong; this we also pray for, that you be made complete.* A prayer for another's spiritual growth.

Eph 6:19 - *and pray on my behalf, that utterance may be given to me in the opening of my mouth, to make known with boldness the mystery of the gospel.* A prayer for another's effectiveness at speaking about Jesus.

Phl 1:9 - *And this I pray, that your love may abound still more and more in real knowledge and all discernment.* A prayer for another's wisdom.

2 Th 1:11 - *To this end also we pray for you always, that our God will count you worthy of your calling, and fulfill every desire for goodness and the work of faith with power.* A prayer that God will work mightily in others.

3 Jn 1:2 - *Beloved, I pray that in all respects you may prosper and be in good health, just as your soul prospers.* A prayer for another's physical and economic well-being.

The content of prayers in these passages, along with the Lord's prayer, can be summed up by saying that any acknowledgement of God's power and sovereignty, and any request for the physical or spiritual well-being of ourselves or others is consistent with biblical teaching.

When I was about 11 years old, I remember hearing a woman say that she prayed every morning to God about which cereal she should eat that day. I also recall thinking to myself that I didn't think God really cared much what cereal this woman actually chose to eat. When we pray, we are praying to the God who created the universe and everything in it. I appreciate that this woman thought she should involve God in every decision she made, whether big or small. But, we are told in Scripture that we should not be concerned about what we eat or what we wear. These are trivial matters when you consider people's souls are at stake. Our thoughts, and our prayer requests, should be geared towards eternally significant matters. That is the example of Scripture. Hearing people ask God to bless their pets or their boats or to entreat God to stop the rain from ruining the company picnic, makes prayer sound like small talk with your neighbor over the back fence. Prayer is a sacred privilege given by God to His children. Let us use it with the appropriate respect and dignity it deserves.

As to whom we should pray to, Scripture is quite clear. All prayer is to be directed to God. In the Old Testament, prayer was offered to God using the Hebrew words "Elohim" or "Adonai" or "Jehovah." Each of these names refer to the one God, creator of the universe.

In the New Testament, prayers are either offered to God the Father, or to Jesus. Stephen, in the midst of being stoned prayed, *"Lord Jesus, receive my spirit"* (Acts 7:59). Since Jesus and the Father are one (Jn 10:30), it makes sense that addressing a prayer to either is addressing a prayer to the same God. We are told that Jesus is the Head of the Church and that He grants us peace (2Th 3:16) and mercy (1Cor 7:25), He blesses us (Rom 10:12), He intercedes for us (Rom 8:35), and He equips the Church (Eph 1:1). Certainly, our Lord desires to hear our prayers and addressing our prayers to Him, or the Father, conforms to biblical teaching.

Nowhere in Scripture is there an example of, or instruction to, pray to any human, either dead or alive. Nowhere. Not one. There are no prayers to Abraham, Isaac, or Jacob, our great Patriarchs. There are no prayers to Moses or Isaiah. There are no prayers to Adam or to Eve, the mother of the human race. No prayers to John the Baptist, of whom Jesus said *"Truly I say to you, among those born of women there has not arisen anyone greater than John the Baptist"* (Mt 11:1). Prayers are reserved for God alone. Praying to anything, or anyone else, is considered idolatry, plain and simple. Our affections and our reliance is to be directed to God alone.

Reconsidering the Hail Mary prayer, one may try to argue that this is not really a prayer at all (although it is called this by most all catholic sources).[1] Maybe it is just a recognition of who Mary is and a fulfillment of the Scripture verses given in Luke. There we read,

"And coming in, he [Gabriel] *said to her* [Mary], *Greetings, favored one, the Lord is with you"* (1:28). And, *"she* [Elizabeth] *cried out with a loud voice and said, 'Blessed are you among women and blessed is the fruit of your womb"* (1:42). And, *"my* [Mary's] *spirit has rejoiced in God my savior. For He has had regard for the humble state of His bondslave; for behold, from this time on all generations will count me blessed"* (1:47,48).

The first half of the Hail Mary prayer is nearly a quote from Scripture and is, in fact, just a pronouncement of the facts. Mary was blessed, she was full of grace, and the fruit of her womb was Jesus. The second portion, the part that appeals to Mary to pray for "us sinners now and at the hour of our death," sounds as if the person doing the asking thinks Mary is in a special place to intercede for us with God.

The Apostle Paul tells us *"For there is one God, and one mediator also between God and men, the man Christ Jesus"* (1Ti 2:5). The Hail Mary recitation is confusing in that it seems to put Mary in the position of mediator between God and men. Yes, it is appropriate to ask for prayer from friends and family for our spiritual well-being now and at the hour of our death. That prayer would be for grace and courage and an unshakable faith. But the invocation to "Holy Mary, Mother of God," implies that her special status gives her special powers of influence. I could be overstating this, but I think not. Ask your Catholic or Orthodox neighbor their understanding of why they pray to Mary.

To be fair, the Catholic and Orthodox Church's official position on prayer to the Saints is that these prayers are always and only requests for intercession - that is, asking them to pray on your behalf - just as you would ask your pastor to pray for you. The problem is that *in practice*, this is not what is being done. Here are a couple of examples of published prayers:

A prayer to St. Gerard

> O good St. Gerard, powerful intercessor before God and wonder worker of our day, confidently *I call upon you* and *seek your aid*. On Earth you always fulfilled God's designs, *help me now* to do the holy will of God.[2]

Another prayer to St. Gerard

> O great St. Gerard, beloved servant of Jesus Christ, perfect imitator of your meek and humble Savior, and devoted child of Mother of God, *enkindle within my heart* one spark of that heavenly fire of charity which glowed in your heart and made you an angel of love.[2]

A prayer to St. Benedict

> Through the cross of Jesus Christ, I ask you to please intercede that God might protect me, my loved ones, my home, property, possessions, and workplace today and always by your holy blessing, that we may never be separated from Jesus, Mary, and the company of all the blessed. Through your intercession may we be delivered from temptation, spiritual oppression, physical ills, and disease. *Protect us from drug and alcohol abuse, impurity and immorality, objectionable companions, and negative attitudes.* In Jesus' Name. Amen.[3]

Note the blurring of distinction between asking the saints to pray on our behalf for something and asking the saint to accomplish the thing in and of themselves. Referring to Saint Gerard as the "perfect imitator" of Jesus elevates him to God status. Also note that separation from Jesus seems to be equated with separation from Mary.

It is only natural, and should be expected, that people who pray to a picture or a statue of a departed human will at some point begin to believe that that person has to power to make things happen for them. The examples above prove the point, official statements to the contrary or not.

All major dictionaries define prayer as a request for help or expression of thanks addressed to God or an object of worship.[4] The Christian Church needs to stop offering prayer to deceased humans because of the inherent and inevitable perception that arises of deifying these brothers and sisters in Christ, whether real or not. It also serves as a false witness to non-Christians who uniformly understand prayer as something directed to Deity.

Prayer should be offered to God and God alone. It should be offered only in an attitude of humility (Mt 6:5), only with a sincere heart (Mt 6:7), and only with faith that God hears and can accomplish all according to His will (Mk 11:24). As Children of God, we are to value prayer as a wonderful privilege and engage in prayer in all places and at all times.

Confession

One of the unfortunate goals some had during the Protestant Reformation was to erase all things Catholic. In regards to confession, Protestants threw the baby out with the bath water.

PRAYER, CONFESSION, FORGIVENESS

If you ask a Protestant what comes to their mind when they hear the words "go to confession," you would likely get a description of a dark and eerie booth, with 2 small doors, set up against a featureless wall. Inside the booth, on the other side of a wood scrolled screen would be the hazy outline of a man, his head tipped back against the wall. Some rote words would be said by the confessor, followed by a recitation of inappropriate behaviors, some mundane, others embarrassingly graphic. After a rather long list of wrongs were enumerated, the faceless person on the other side of the screen would utter a few verses from Scripture, and state "I absolve you of your sins", and would encourage a change of behavior. He would sometimes give the confessor of list of things he must do to make amends.

Is this how confession is supposed to be done?

In the Protestant churches that I grew up in, individual confession was never encouraged. Sure, if someone wanted to meet individually with the pastor to make a confession, it would be welcomed. But, this was rarely done. The expectation was that confession would be done corporately. In some churches this was done by reciting a confession written in the bulletin. It was a generic sort of thing. Statements about all being sinners and needing the grace of God. After the recitation the pastor would then read another statement announcing our forgiveness. In other churches I've been to, confession is done during a quiet moment. The need for confession is stated and then the pastor asks the congregation to confess to God their individual sins silently, in their heads. After 30 seconds or so, the pastor breaks the silence and reads an assurance of God's forgiveness from the bulletin. Some churches just skip it altogether.

Is this how confession is supposed to be done? What does Scripture say?

Unlike the many verses given to us regarding prayer, only a handful of verses instruct us about the meaning and practice of confession. There are 14 in all, 10 in the Old Testament and 4 in the New. These will all be considered.

> 1. Lev 5:5 - *So it shall be when he becomes guilty in one of these, that he shall confess that in which he has sinned.*

This is the first use of the word "confess" in Scripture. The "he" in this verse is anyone who commits a sin or becomes unclean without knowing it, but then gains knowledge of their wrongdoing. They are to confess, and then offer a guilt offering for their sin. Confession is a required part of the forgiveness process. Verse 10 ends the section by stating, *"and it will be forgiven him."*

> 2. Lev 16:21 - *Then Aaron shall lay both of his hands on the head of the live goat, and confess over it all the iniquities of the sons of Israel, and all their transgressions in regard to all their sins.*

This verse comes in the middle of a long chapter about atoning for the sins of Israel. It describes the scapegoat, the animal that has the sins of the nation of Israel placed on its head before being chased out of town. We are told that Aaron is to confess over it all the iniquities of Israel. We are not told how long this takes or exactly how he manages this enormous task. It is important to note that God wants him to verbalize the sins of the people. God knows what these sins are. He doesn't need to hear them. The reason for the enumeration of Israel's sins must be for the wellbeing of the people. Once again, this is part of the forgiveness process.

> 3. Lev 26:40, 42 - *If they confess their iniquity and the iniquity of their forefathers, in their unfaithfulness that*

they committed against me, and also in their acting with hostility against Me - then I will remember My covenant with Jacob, and I will remember also My covenant with Isaac, and My covenant with Abraham as well, and I will remember the land.

The incredible power of confession is highlighted in these verses. In Leviticus 26 God warns Israel that His blessings are dependent on their obedience to the law. If they ignore or willfully transgress His rules, He will allow terrible hardships and suffering to come upon them. However, "if they confess their iniquity," His anger and hostility will cease and He will remember His covenants of blessing. Confession of sin was the key. Confession can also be made for the sins of others, especially our ancestors.

4. Num 5:7 - *Speak to the sons of Israel, "When a man or woman commits any of the sins of mankind, acting unfaithfully against the Lord, and that person is guilty, then he shall confess his sins which he has committed, and he shall make restitution in full for his wrong, and add to it one-fifth of it, and give it to him who he has wronged.*

Why not just pay back a person for the loss that they suffer when wronged? Why make this person verbally confess the sin before making restitution? What does this accomplish? Confession is hard. It would be so much easier to just open your wallet and pay some money. Confession means calling yourself out for wrongdoing. It means owning your transgression. It is humbling and often embarrassing. It is also commanded by God.

5. Neh 1:6 - *let Your ear now be attentive and Your eyes open to hear the prayer of Your servant which I am praying before you now, day and night, on behalf of the*

sons of Israel your servants, confessing the sins of the sons of Israel, which we have sinned against you; I and my father's house have sinned.

Confessing to God the sins of those with whom you live and identify with is biblical. Including yourself in the confession is expected.

> 6. Ps 32:5 - *I acknowledged my sin to You, and my iniquity I did not hide; I said, "I will confess my transgression to the Lord;" and You forgave the guilt of my sin.*

Once again, confession is seen clearly linked to forgiveness. Nothing else is mentioned as a prerequisite or requirement.

> 7. Ps 38:18 - *For I confess my iniquity; I am full of anxiety because of my sin.*

In this Psalm from David, he cries out to God for aid. He is oppressed by his sin and feels threatened by his enemies. In the midst of his anguish he remembers to confess his sin. He is a king. He answers to no human. Yet he realizes confession before God will bring relief to his soul.

> 8. Prov 28:13 - *He who conceals his transgressions will not prosper, but he who confesses and forsakes them will find compassion.*

Solomon includes words of wisdom regarding confession. Not only is confession answered by God with forgiveness, compassion is also awarded to those who reveal their errors.

> 9. Dan 9:20 - *Now while I was speaking and praying, and confessing my sin and the sin of my people Israel, and presenting my supplication before the Lord my God in behalf of the holy mountain of my God,*

Daniel includes confession for himself and his people alongside his requests. God honors his prayers with a vision about the future. In the preceding verses, Daniel laments that *"open shame belongs to us, O Lord, to our kings, our princes and our fathers, because we have sinned against You."* Daniel, the one faithful even unto death, repeatedly includes himself in confessing his people's sin.

> 10. Mar 1:5 - *And all the country of Judea was going out to him, and all the people in Jerusalem; and they were being baptized by him in the Jordan River, confessing their sins.*

John the Baptist came *"preaching a baptism of repentance for the forgiveness of sins"* (v 4). This repentance included confession of sin. Before someone can turn away (repent) from their ungodly behaviors, they first need to identify what those behaviors are. It does little good to say "I'll make a commitment to change" when it is not clear what exactly you need to change. Confessing one's sins allows accountability to occur.

> 11. Acts 19:18 - *Many also of those who had believed kept coming, confessing and disclosing their practices.*

The "many" in this verse are the people in Asia who have heard the Apostle Paul preach the gospel and seen him demonstrate Jesus' power by the performing of miracles. These people were both *"Jews and Greeks"* (v 19). Their confession seemed to be ongoing. These are people who *"had believed"* and *"kept coming."* Confession was not something to be done just once, at their baptism or conversion.

> 12. James 5:16 - *Therefore, confess your sins to one another, and pray for one another that you may be healed. The effective prayer of a righteous man can accomplish much.*

James has just given instruction about gathering the elders to pray for someone who is ill. He states that the prayer offered in faith will bring both physical and spiritual healing. Confession of sins, *one to another,* is to be part of this process. In the Old Testament verses, confession to God is either stated or implied. In these New Testament verses, there is more of a sense of confessing our sins to a brother or sister in Christ. This verse makes it explicit. Along with confession of sin to God, we are also to confess our sin to one another. This must be done out loud, to another sinful human, putting at risk our reputation and our righteous facade.

13. 1 John 1:9 - *If we confess our sins, He is faithful and righteous to forgive us our sins and to cleanse us from all unrighteousness.*

The "if, then" structure of this verse is striking. "If" we confess our sins … The implications are very important for understanding forgiveness. What about sins we don't confess? Do these go unforgiven? Isn't forgiveness based on our faith, apart from anything we actually do? (For answers to these, see the next section) We can at least say that God honors confession with forgiveness. Confession results in God cleansing *"us from all unrighteousness."*

The fact that there are only four verses in the New Testament about confession in relation to sin could lead one to believe it must not be that important. On the contrary, the New Testament verses confirm what the Old Testament teaches. They demonstrate continuity between the practices of the Old Covenant in terms of confession, with that of the New. We are still to confess our sin; it is still related to forgiveness of our sin; and, we are to confess our sin both to God and to one another.

PRAYER, CONFESSION, FORGIVENESS

If we Christians took confession seriously, as Scripture indicates we should, confession would be breaking out all over. I expect half our prayers would be committed to confession. Our conversations with others would be sprinkled with confessions of our greed, pride, and coveting. Pastors and priests would need to enlist lay persons to handle all the requests from people wanting to confess their sin.

The corporate confession that Protestant churches engage in (if they do it at all) is generally anemic and superficial. It is forced and contrived. When I am told to pause and confess my sins to God in the middle of a church service, half the time my mind wanders to consider what I plan to get done the rest of the day (my confession). I doubt that I am alone. Yes, it does make me consider for a few moments what big things I may have done wrong in the past week, but, honestly, the 30 or 45 seconds we are given to conjure up these confessions betrays the church's true feeling about the importance of confession. And for good reason. The Protestant church, in its zeal to not be Catholic, reworked the teaching on forgiveness which makes confession optional - not a required part of a Christian's life. An encouraged practice, to be sure, but not anything that impacts our relationship to God.

The Catholic and Orthodox churches, to their credit, expect and teach that confession is an essential part of the believer's life. Their practice of referring all confession to a priest, however, is not supported by Scripture. Confession can be made to any person - God's forgiveness is not dependent on who hears the confession, but on the state of the confessor's heart (Ps 51:17). The early church's establishment of the confession booth was an understandable attempt to focus attention on this practice, to regulate its use, and to provide a safe place to participate. There is nothing wrong with the use of a confession booth, and for some, it is the place that provides the greatest spiritual comfort.

Martin Luther began his 95 theses by stating, "When our Lord and Master Jesus Christ said, 'Repent,' he willed the entire life of a believer to be one of repentance." Repentance begins with confession. My prayer for the Body of Christ is that it rededicates itself to valuing and practicing biblical confession.

Forgiveness

The Parable of the Twin Brothers

There once were two boys, twins, who were 10 years old. One Saturday morning, their mother announced to them after breakfast that the day had come for their older sister to be married. She dressed each of the boys in new white play clothes and told them that the adults would be spending the day preparing for the evening wedding. They could do as they please for the whole day. She had only two requests. The first was that they were to try hard to keep their new outfits clean. The second was that they were to meet their father at the rear door of the church at 5 pm to get ready for the ceremony.

The boys were ecstatic. Both loved to play outside and each envisioned a grand day of exploring in the woods, playing hide and seek, and hanging out in their treehouse. Just before leaving the house, their mother handed each of them a small round tube, like a large chap stick. She told them, "This is a special clothing stick. If you happen to get any dirt on your clothes or if you spill something, quickly rub this on the spot and it will immediately disappear." The boys each dropped the stick into their front pocket and headed off.

One of the brothers took his mother's instructions very

seriously. He frequently checked his clothes for any marks and when he spotted one, he used the special stick his mother had given him. It worked! Knowing that he could keep his clothes clean in this way actually freed him to run and jump and play all the harder. He did, occasionally, cause his brother and their friends to pause while he checked himself out and used his stain remover, but in his mind it was well worth it. He even asked his friends a couple of times throughout the day to check out his back since he couldn't really see it. By mid-afternoon, he was still going strong with a surprisingly clean set of clothes on his back.

The other brother seemed to not care too much about his new clothes. When he got the first few smudges on the pant legs, he decided it really wasn't all that bad. Certainly he didn't need to stop what he was doing to clean up a few spots. When he saw his brother diligently using his stick to keep himself clean, he thought to himself that it seemed a waste of time. He knew his father would let them into the wedding regardless of how dirty their clothes were. He loved them, didn't he? And besides, they were boys. They were supposed to get dirty, right?

By midafternoon, the apathetic brother started to feel a bit uneasy. His clothes were now quite filthy. He hadn't used his stick once and it was getting hard to tell if his clothes were supposed to be white or brown or green or some combination of the three. The words of his mother echoed in his head. A creeping feeling of guilt kept intruding on his fun and his irritability prompted his friends to ask more than once what was wrong. At this point, he figured it was too late to even try to do anything about his appearance. There was so much dirt on his clothes, how could his mom's little stick do any real good.

Just before 5 pm, the two boys started to head to the church. One of the brothers had on nearly new looking play clothes -

there were just a few, barely noticeable traces of dirt on the left pant leg and behind the right shoulder. This boy was skipping to the church, smiling, and thinking that he had just had the best day ever. The other brother was a mess. He walked slowly with his eyes fixed on the ground just in front of his feet. He was trying to decide if he should even show up to the church. Would his father let him in? What would he say? He thought about how much fun this day was supposed to be. His brother sure seemed to enjoy it. He just felt awful.

The boy's father was waiting for them at the back door of the church when they arrived. One was all grins, the other all gloom. The father spent a moment glancing from one boy to the other with understanding eyes. He then reached over to the coat rack on his right and produced 2 identical white choir robes. He handed one to each of his sons saying, "Welcome my sons," gave them a hug, and told them to put it on over their play clothes. At once they donned their robes and went in, one boy feeling quite relieved, the other feeling quite blessed.

The vast majority of Protestant churches teach that at the instant a person comes to faith, or "gets saved", all sin, past, present, and future, is forgiven. This teaching is inconsistent, confusing, and dangerous, besides being just not true.

It is inconsistent in that these churches all affirm the ancient Nicene Creed, which states, "I believe in one baptism for the remission of sin." If faith comes prior to baptism, and all sins are forgiven at the instant one comes to faith, then there would be no sins for the baptism to remit. It is confusing because these same churches ask God for forgiveness when they pray the Lord's prayer and are told if they confess their sin, God is faithful to forgive that sin. But I thought their sin had already been forgiven? It is dangerous because this teaching promotes spiritual malaise and a callous disregard for sin. Why be concerned about any sin you might commit in the future if it has already been forgiven?

Where does this teaching come from? Are there any verses that say such a thing?

No, there aren't.

The verses that are generally quoted to justify this position are those that have the words "all" and "sin" in them. The one that comes to mind first is 1 John 1:7:

But if we walk in the Light as He Himself is in the Light, we have fellowship with one another, and the blood of Jesus Christ cleanses us from all sin.

As is always the case when trying to get at the best meaning of a verse, the question that needs to be asked is, what is the Spirit trying to teach us? Is God wanting to teach us about the timing of forgiveness? Is He saying that as soon as we start walking "in the Light" that we are cleansed "from all sin?" Or does our walking in the Light *"cleanse us from all sin,"* past, present and future? Or maybe the point is that the blood of Jesus is sufficient to handle all our sins, no matter their severity.

Reading a little further in this chapter helps to clarify John's meaning. In the next 2 verses he says,

If we say that we have no sin, we are deceiving ourselves, and the truth is not in us. If we confess our sins, he is faithful and just to forgive us our sins and cleanse us from all unrighteousness.

These verses make no sense for the Children of God if all sin is forgiven at conversion. John makes the point that all disciples of Christ continue to have sin that needs to be forgiven. Confession is one means to obtain that forgiveness. Christ's blood is sufficient to forgive any and all sin, to *"cleanse us from all unrighteousness."* There are no sins that are beyond the forgiveness made available through Jesus' sacrifice.

Romans 6:10 says, *"For the death that He died, He died to sin once for all; but the life that He lives, He lives for God."* This phrase, *"died to sin once for all,"* is repeated in 1 Peter 3:18. Timing is again the question. Does this phrase mean when Jesus died, all sin that all future Christians would ever commit was forgiven? Or does it mean Christ's death, and the shedding of His blood, was the one truly effective sacrifice for all sin? That no further sacrifices would ever be needed to atone for humanity's sin? The latter would be the correct meaning if the rest of Scripture teaches us that forgiveness is an ongoing activity.

Jesus' own words confirm the ongoing need for forgiveness, even after conversion. In Mark 2 we are told the famous story of the paralytic being lowered through the roof by his friends. Scripture tells us, *"And Jesus, seeing their faith, said to the paralytic, 'Son, your sins are forgiven'"* (v 5).

Now, what just happened here? Did Jesus actually forgive this man's sins when He said that, or was He merely announcing to him that His sins had been forgiven at some point in the past, when he came to faith?

He didn't come to faith at the moment he saw Jesus - he and his friends would not have made the effort to dig through the roof overhead and lower him down into the crowd had they not had faith in Jesus. The Scribes made it clear what they thought: *"Why does this man speak that way? He is blaspheming; only God can forgive sins"* (v 7). Jesus responds to them by asserting

His power to forgive sin, *"But so that you may know that the Son of Man has authority on earth to forgive sins - He said to the paralytic, 'I say to you, get up, pick up your pallet and go home'"* (v 10,11). This man's sin was forgiven by Jesus just prior to his physical healing.

In Luke 11, Jesus is teaching His disciples to pray. He tells them that when they pray they should say,

> *"Father, hallowed be Your name. Your kingdom come. Give us each day our daily bread. And forgive us our sins, for we ourselves also forgive everyone who is indebted to us"* (v 2-4).

Jesus tells us to pray to the Father to forgive our sins. Again, this would make absolutely no sense if all our sins had already been forgiven. It also means that forgiveness is granted to those who pray for it, in faith. Jesus would not teach us to ask the Father for something that He is unwilling or unable to grant. Forgiveness of sins comes to those disciples of Christ who confess their sin, and also to those who humbly ask God to forgive their sin.

What about Romans 8:1: *"There is now no condemnation for those who are in Christ."* If we Christians are walking around with unforgiven sin because we haven't specifically prayed for forgiveness for that sin or confessed it, doesn't that mean that if we die we do not have the righteousness of Christ which is necessary for admittance into heaven?

Absolutely not! The Apostle Paul says that yes, we still sin (Rom 7:19), even though our baptism into Christ has buried the sinful nature (Rom 6:4-6), and yes, we pursue and receive justification, (being declared righteous) throughout our lives of faith on this earth (Gal 2:17, Phl 3:12), waiting for the day when we will be made complete. Thanks be to God, when we come before the Eternal Judge, we will be perfected by being covered with the full righteousness of Christ (Phl 3:20-21).

The parable of the twin brothers is of course an analogy of the Christian life. The new, clean play clothes that the boys receive represent the results of their baptism into Christ. Their Saturday is their life of freedom, to do and experience freely the fullness of God's creation. Dirt is sin, and their mother's instructions to stay clean mirrors our Lord's instructions to us to *"be holy yourselves, also in all your behavior"* (1 Pet 1:15). The stain removing clothing stick represents God's gifts to us of prayer, confession, and other activities that are credited to us as righteousness (see chapter 10). The wedding celebration is the prophesied heavenly wedding celebration, when Christ will be united with His bride, the Church.

But what of faith? Where is faith in this portrayal?

Faith is what got these boys into this family. Faith is what allowed this Father to welcome his sons into the wedding feast, despite their less than perfect appearance. Faith is what bought the choir robes for the boys to wear. And faith is what sealed their adoption as sons - neither was born into this family.

If both brothers were allowed into the wedding, then what difference, really, did the diligent brother's obedience make?

It made a difference in many ways. The diligent brother's life experience was one of freedom from guilt and remorse. He served as an example to those around him. He was able to make decisions knowing that if he slipped, there was provision for him to repair any damage. Lastly, when his father welcomed them into the wedding, there would be an expectation that the diligent son would be given a leading role in the proceedings. He had demonstrated a level of faithfulness that would be rewarded.

PRAYER, CONFESSION, FORGIVENESS

Such an understanding of the Christian life makes sense of a passage in Scripture I had always wondered about. In 1 Corinthians, the Apostle Paul says,

Now if any man builds on the foundation [Jesus Christ] *with gold, silver, precious stones, wood, hay, straw, each man's work will become evident; for the day will show it because it is to be revealed with fire, and the fire itself will test the quality of each man's work. For if any man's work which he has built on it remains, he will receive a reward. If any man's work is burned up, he will suffer loss; but he himself will be saved, yet so as through fire (3:12-15).*

Not all Christians will arrive at the door of the wedding feast on equal footing. Some will be recognized for their life well lived, while others will gain access as one who escapes a collapsing building.

Jesus Christ died once for the sins of all. Forgiveness is available to all who believe and trust in Him. God asks us to demonstrate our trust by participating in prayer and confession, and promises His real and complete forgiveness in return. The righteousness of Christ, given to all who believe and trust in Him, is our only, and sure, hope for acceptance into God's eternal kingdom.

11

Good Works and Holy Living

The five solas: Sola Scriptura, Sola Fide, Sola Gratia, Solus Christus, and Soli Deo Gloria. The foundation stones of the Protestant Reformation. Scripture alone, faith alone, grace alone, Christ alone, to the Glory of God alone.

Growing up in the Lutheran Church, I heard a lot about how these five descriptors explained our Christian faith. I also got an earful about how the Catholic Church had strayed from these principles, especially Sola Fide - faith alone. I was told that the Catholic Church had for centuries embraced "works righteousness" and that this was a heresy, bringing into question their right to even call themselves Christian. Needless to say, we didn't pray, worship, or really even associate with any Catholics, except for my Aunt who had converted from Lutheranism to Catholicism when she got married. This was always a sore point for my parents, and a curiosity for me.

As I got into my teens and started to think through what I was being taught in Sunday School, I became aware of 2 huge problems with the "faith alone" dogma.

The first of these involves what I believe to be the most glaring, apparent inconsistency in the entire New Testament. If you search for the phrase "faith alone" in Scripture, it occurs only once. At the end of James chapter 2, James, the brother of Jesus, concludes after discussing the role of works in justification:

You see that a man is justified by works, and not by faith alone (v 24).

It is strikingly ironic that in the only place that "faith alone" occurs in Scripture, it contradicts the very teaching the Protestant Church says is the most (or at least among the most) important. And, it remains one of the main sticking points in conversations between Catholics and Protestants trying to find common ground.

This James verse seems to directly contradict the Apostle Paul's teaching to the Galatians:

Nevertheless, knowing that a man is not justified by the works of the law but by faith in Christ Jesus, even we have believed in Christ Jesus, so that we may be justified by faith in Christ and not by the works of the law, since by the works of the law no flesh will be justified. (Gal 2:16)

There it is. Two verses that appear to teach opposite truths. James says that men are justified by works, at least in addition to faith, while Paul says by works no man will be justified. This apparent contradiction must be resolved in a way that is faithful to both verses without doing unreasonable gymnastics with the language or meanings to get there.

The second big problem with "faith alone" is the issue of God's judgement. Jesus used many parables to teach His followers. One of the more well-known is the parable of the sheep and the goats. He introduces the topic of the Final Judgement in verse 31 of Matthew 25:

But when the Son of Man comes in His glory, and all the angels with Him, then He will sit on His glorious throne. All the nations will be gathered before Him; and He will separate them one from another, like a shepherd separates the sheep from the goats; and He will put the sheep on His right, and the goats on His left. Then the King will say to those on His right, "Come, you who are blessed of My Father, inherit the kingdom prepared for you from the foundation of the world."

Beautiful, exciting, and comforting words every human longs to hear. Clearly Jesus is telling us what to expect when that great and terrible day, the Day of the Lord, arrives.

The next words we might expect the King to say to those inheriting the kingdom would be something like, "For you kept the faith to the end. You accepted as truth the sacrifice of the Lamb of God, whose blood now covers all your unrighteousness. Enter into your rest."

He does not commend their faith. Instead, He tells them:

For I was hungry and you gave me something to eat; I was thirsty and you gave me something to drink; I was a stranger and you invited Me in; naked and you clothed me; I was sick and you visited Me; I was in prison and you came to Me. Then the righteous will answer Him, Lord, when did we see You hungry and feed you, or thirsty, and give You something to drink? And when did we see You a stranger, and invite You in, or naked, and clothe You? When did we see You sick or in prison, and come to You? The King will answer and say to them, "Truly I say to You, to the extent that you did it to one of these brothers of Mine, even the least of them, you did it to Me." (v 35-40)

Amazing. The Lord divides the nations into the saved and the condemned, and He gives as his reasoning their good works. Plain and simple. He continues on and says to those destined for hell that they did not feed or clothe or house or visit *"one of the least of these."* They will be thrown into the lake of fire.

I called this the parable of the sheep and goats, but that is not correct. This teaching is not a parable. It's not a story about sheep and goats that is somehow an analogy to humanity. This teaching is just a straightforward explanation from Jesus about what will take place at the resurrection of the living and the dead. There's really no room for dickering about interpretation. Whether or not Jesus will say those exact words to the two groups of people isn't the point. The Spirit is conveying to us through the text that we will be judged based on our works.

This is not what I was taught from the pulpit week after week growing up, or since for that matter. Rather the opposite - good works are nice, but they have no bearing on my salvation.

As I started to seek out other Scripture about Judgement Day, it became clear that this text's message was the rule rather than the exception. God will judge us based on our actions and behaviors, not some inward, invisible faith.

Jer 17:10 I, the Lord, search the heart, I test the mind, even to give to each man according to his ways, according to the results of his deeds.

Ez 33:20 the Lord says, "O house of Israel, I will judge each of you according to his ways."

Mat 16:27 Jesus says, "For the Son of Man is going to come in the glory of His Father with His angels, and will then repay every man according to his deeds."

John 5:28,29 Do not marvel at this; for an hour is coming, in which all who are in the tombs will hear His voice, and will come forth; those who did the good deeds to a resurrection of life, those who committed the evil deeds to a resurrection of judgement.

Rom 2:6 But because of your stubbornness and unrepentant heart you are storing up wrath for yourself in the day of wrath and revelation of the righteous judgement of God, who will render unto each person according to his deeds.

2 Cor 5:10 For we must all appear before the judgement seat of Christ, so that each one may be recompensed for his deeds in the body, according to what he has done whether good or bad.

Gal 6:7-8 Do not be deceived, God is not mocked; for whatever a man sows, this he will also reap. For the one who sows to his own flesh will from the flesh reap corruption, but the one who sows to the Spirit will from the Spirit reap eternal life.

Eph 5:6 after describing the evil deeds of the wicked, Paul warns, "Let no one deceive you with empty words, for because of these things the wrath of God comes upon the sons of disobedience.

Rev 20:12 at the great white throne of judgement, "the dead were judged from the things which were written in the books, according to their deeds."

Rev 22:12 Jesus says, "Behold, I am coming quickly, and My reward is with Me, to render to every man according to what he has done."

These verses represent a partial list of verses showing the pervasiveness and consistency of God's criteria for our judgement.

So, how is this to be resolved? Are we saved by faith or by our works? Why does the New Testament teaching on salvation seem so inconsistent? Is it faith *and* works? The Apostle Paul so adamantly teaches we are saved by faith, apart from works (Eph 2:8,9). Are good works essential to our salvation?

To unravel this conundrum, we must first acknowledge that all "works" are not the same. The Scriptures talk about 4 distinct, very different, kinds of works.

1. Works of the law - actions and behaviors which are done, apart from any faith in Jesus, that are meant to demonstrate obedience to God's law or to display our inherent goodness, thus earning favor from God (self-merited righteousness).
2. Works of faith - actions and behaviors which are done at God's request, fully believing and trusting in the promises of God, without expectation of self-earned merit. These actions involve some personal risk.
3. Evil Works - actions and behaviors that are done to benefit self, often associated with causing harm to others.
4. Good Works - actions and behaviors that are done to benefit others, motivated by the desire to bring glory to God. These actions involve some degree of self-sacrifice.

God does not lump these together into one all-inclusive category called "works," nor does He respond to them in the same way. Unfortunately, my experience is that the Protestant church rarely differentiates between these clearly different types of works when it discusses the subject. Scripture often specifies exactly which kind of works are being referenced, but not always. When the word "works" occurs by itself, it is imperative to figure out which kind the writer is talking about.

For example, in Gal 2:16 (see above), Paul makes it very clear, by repeating it over and over, that he is talking about *"works of the law."* In James 2:24, James uses the word "works" without a qualifier. What kind of works is he talking about? He references Abraham offering up Isaac as a sacrifice and Rahab risking her life to save Jewish spies sent by God. These are works of faith. Abraham was willing to offer up the life of Isaac to God because he trusted that God would honor His promise of an heir, *"and it was reckoned to him as righteousness"* (Ja 2:23). It was not reckoned to him as righteousness because he physically brought Isaac to the place of sacrifice, or because he was willing to drop the knife. No, it was reckoned to him as righteousness because he trusted in God and the promises of God.

For some works, it is clear what category the work fits into. Murdering your neighbor to gain his wife is an evil work. Other works can be less clear. The underlying reason behind the action being taken is the key.

You would think prayer to God would be a work of faith. Jesus teaches us this is not necessarily so. He tells the story of 2 men who approach God in prayer:

> *Two men went up into the temple to pray, one a Pharisee and the other a tax collector. The Pharisee stood and*

was praying this to himself: "God, I thank you that I am not like other people, swindlers, unjust, adulterers, or even like this tax collector. I fast twice a week; I pay tithes of all that I get." But the tax collector, standing some distance away, was even unwilling to lift up his eyes to heaven, but was beating his breast saying, "God, be merciful to me, the sinner." I tell you, this man went to his house justified rather than the other. (Luk 18:10-14)

Two men are considered, each doing the same action, praying. One went home justified, declared righteous, while the other did not. Why? Because one prayer was a work of faith while the other was a work of the law.

Was the tax collector justified before he said his prayer, or after? This might seem like an odd question but it is vitally important to the topic of works righteousness. Protestants would be compelled to answer "before," because any hint of a work being related to justification might somehow detract from "faith alone." Catholics and Orthodox would say "after," without much hesitation. Given the text, it does seem "after" would be the more natural, straight forward understanding of Jesus' words, *"this man went to his house justified."*

The passage that most Protestant pastors will head to to show that justification is not related to the occurrence of a work is Romans 4. There the Apostle Paul continues his argument that man is justified by faith, apart from the *"works of the law"* (3:28), by using Abraham and circumcision as an example. Starting at chapter 4, verse 8 he quotes David saying, *"Blessed is the man whose sin the Lord will not take into account."* He then continues,

Is this blessing then on the circumcised, or on the uncircumcised also? For we say, 'Faith was credited to Abraham as righteousness.' How then was it credited? While he was circumcised or uncircumcised? Not while circumcised, but while uncircumcised; and he received the sign of circumcision, a seal of the righteousness of the faith which he had while uncircumcised, so that he might be the father of all who believe without being circumcised, that righteousness might be credited to them, and the father of circumcision to those who not only are of the circumcision, but who also follow in the steps of the faith of our father Abraham, which he had while uncircumcised. (v 9-12)

In sorting out the meaning of this verse, first note that Paul's main purpose is to answer the question about whose sin the Lord will not take into account. That is, who will be declared righteous before God. Second, Paul's explanation here continues his thoughts on righteousness derived by works of the law. How do we know? Because Paul says *"works of the law"* twice in the preceding verses (3:20 and 28) just to be sure we are clear about what kind of work he is talking about. Third, this is not about *when* a person is justified, but *how* a person is justified. We know that because Paul specifically says, *"How then was it [righteousness] credited?"* So this passage has nothing to do with justification associated with works of faith or good works. Nor is it about the timing of justification. To make it about either of those two things is forcing a meaning onto a verse that it *explicitly* says it is not about. This verse is about justification apart from the works of the law. Paul uses the act of circumcision to emphasize that non-Jews will be justified by their faith, apart from this work, just as Jews will be justified by faith, even though circumcised. Their going through circumcision, a painful activity mind you, does not merit their righteousness.

Imagine Abraham responding to God, after God told him to pack up his family and move to another country, "God, I certainly believe in you. And I trust that you would take care of my family and me. And I even trust that you would give me and my descendants a land to live in for a long, long time. But, I'm just not feeling it right now. I think I will stay put, trusting that you will take care of me and my family here in Heron." Would we expect God's response to be, "And Abraham's faith was credited to him as righteousness?" Of course not.

Throughout this book I have argued that faith has 2 components, belief and trust. The currency of faith is a coin, with belief on one side and trust on the other.[1] Belief is something we hold in our head. Trust must be demonstrated. It is something all can see. It was trust that caused Noah to build an ark, awaiting the promised flood. It was trust in God and the promises of God that allowed Abraham to be willing to offer his son as a sacrifice. It was trust that allowed Rahab to risk her life to save the Jewish spies. It was trust that allowed Moses to stand before Pharaoh and pronounce plague after plague. It is trust in the promises of God that impels parents to bring their infant forward for baptism into Christ for the forgiveness of sins. It takes trust to confess the Lord Jesus Christ in a crowd hostile to the Gospel.

All these works of faith are associated with the bestowing of the righteousness of Christ. James makes this connection clear:

> *Was not Abraham our father justified [declared righteous] by works when he offered up Isaac his son on the altar? You see that faith was working with his works, and as a result of his works, faith was perfected (2:21,22).*

The writer of Hebrews 11, the faith chapter, says the same thing. After listing off all the courageous and sacrificial things the people of God have done, making sure to emphasize these were works of faith by specifically saying each was done *"in faith,"* he states, *"And all these [people - Abraham, Moses, Rahab], have gained approval through their faith" (Heb 11:39).*

Having made the distinction between works of the law and works of faith, the right question to ask may not be, "Do Catholics believe in works righteousness?" The more important question may be, "Do Protestants really reject works righteousness?"

The Bible clearly teaches that the righteousness of Christ is **not** granted through works of the law, but **is** granted through works of faith. The teaching and examples given in Scripture that defend this statement are specific, plentiful, and consistent. And, as hard as it may be for some Protestants to accept, this doesn't invalidate "faith alone." Technically, this is still true. Any work that is done without faith, not for the purpose of glorifying God, is not a work of faith or a good work.

In the middle of Hebrews chapter 11, the writer pauses to let us know that if any of the works that he is reciting were done without faith, they would not have gained God's approval: *"And without faith it is impossible to please Him, for he who comes to God must believe that He is and that He is a rewarder of those who seek Him" (v 6).*

The problem with continuing to use the term "faith alone" is that most people hear "belief alone." There is a (Protestant) understanding that what a person does after conversion, his works, are really not that important because, after all, our justification comes all at once at the moment we come to faith. Our works aren't a part of the "faith" that "alone" allows us to be called "righteous" by God (Mat 25:37). This encourages and excuses an unproductive Christian life.

This is a damaging, and potentially damning, error to believe. James, the brother of Jesus, tells us why.

Apparently there were a group people calling themselves followers of Jesus who were not displaying the fruits of the spirit in their daily lives. They were listening to the words of the teachers, and said they believed, but were showing partiality to the rich, allowing ungodly words to dominate their conversation, and were displaying no compassion to those in need. James chides these people saying, *"prove yourselves doers of the word, and not merely hearers who delude themselves" (1:22)*. He goes on to challenge this group,

> *What use is it, my brethren, if someone says he has faith but has no works? Can that faith save him? Even so, faith without works is dead, being by itself (2:14,17).*

True faith, the faith that comes from having the Spirit of God dwell in our hearts, has a component of trust that is manifested by works of faith and good works. That's because faith is more than just belief. James says just that: *"You believe that God is One. You do well; the demons also believe and shudder. But are you willing to recognize, you foolish fellow, that faith without works is useless" (2:19,20)*?

So does the Catholic Church get this right? Do they teach that justification comes only through faith, demonstrated through works, and that there is no merit on our part; that we in no way earn our salvation? Not growing up in the Catholic Church I have to rely on their official statements of doctrine. Reviewing what is said about justification in the Catholic Catechism we read:

1. The grace of the Holy Spirit has the power to justify us, that is, to cleanse us from our sins and to communicate to us "the righteousness of God through faith in Jesus Christ."
2. Through the power of the Holy Spirit we take part in Christ's Passion by dying to sin, and in His Resurrection by being born to a new life; we are members of his Body which is the Church, branches grafted onto the vine of Himself.
3. The first work of the grace of the Holy Spirit is conversion, effecting justification in accordance with Jesus' proclamation at the beginning of the Gospel: "Repent, for the kingdom of heaven is at hand.
4. Justification detaches man from sin which contradicts the love of God, and purifies his heart of sin.
5. Justification is at the same time the acceptance of God's righteousness through faith in Jesus Christ.
6. Justification has been merited for us by the Passion of Christ who offered himself on the cross a living victim, holy and pleasing to God, and whose blood has become the instrument of atonement for the sins of all men.[2]

This does not sound like justification apart from faith, or "works righteousness." Faith in Jesus is repeatedly given as the reason for our justification.

If this were where it ended, I don't think there would be disagreement within the Church. Unfortunately, shortly after these statements on justification are recorded, the issue of "merit" is raised. Starting with a definition, the pertinent statements read:

GOOD WORKS AND HOLY LIVING

1. The term "merit" refers in general to the recompense owed by a community or a society for the action of one of its members, experienced either as beneficial or harmful, deserving reward or punishment.
2. With regard to God, there is no strict right to any merit on the part of man. [So far so good]
3. The merit of man before God in the Christian life arises from the fact that God has freely chosen to associate man with the work of His grace. The fatherly action of God is first on His own initiative, and then follows man's free acting through his collaboration, so that the merit of good works is to be attributed in the first place to the grace of God, then to the faithful. [This sounds like a move toward attributing merit to man]
4. Filial adoption, in making us partakers by grace in the divine nature, can bestow true merit on us as a result of God's gratuitous justice. This is our right by grace, the full right of love, making us "co-heirs" with Christ and worthy of obtaining "the promised inheritance of eternal life." [With the use of the words "right" and "worthy," this has become a dangerous statement]
5. Since the initiative belongs to God in the order of grace, no one can merit the initial grace of forgiveness and justification, at the beginning of conversion. Moved by the Holy Spirit and charity, *we can then merit for ourselves and for others the graces needed for our sanctification, for the increase of grace and charity, and for the attainment of eternal life.*[3] *[my emphasis]*

This last statement is just plain false and a contradiction of the Christian doctrine of salvation through the merits of Christ alone. It's very unfortunate that this section was even written. Deleting it from the Catholic Catechism would in no way harm the Gospel of Jesus Christ and would make consistent the message that salvation comes through the righteousness of Christ alone, applied to those who are called according to His purpose and do His will (Mat 7:21).

Protestant theologians have understandably feared attaching God's justification to any human work, even works of faith, due to the inclination of man to take credit. The Catholic statements on merit bear this out. Yet, fear must not keep us from speaking the truth. God declares us righteous, wiping our slate clean, through faithful participation in prayer (Luk 18:14), baptism (Acts 22:16), confession (1Jn 1:9), other works of faith (Jam 2:22, Mat 5:10), and good works (Mat 25:34-36). Justification is not a process, but a recurring event, meant to continually refresh and renew His bride. We need to combat the error of self-righteousness by persistently pointing to the cross, not by ignoring or trying to explain away straightforward biblical passages.

Holy Living

How does holy living fit into this explanation of works?

The Apostle Peter tells us, *"As obedient children, do not be conformed to the former lusts which were yours in your ignorance, but like the Holy One who called you, be holy yourselves also in all your behavior"* (1Pet 1:14,15). The Apostle Paul further exhorts us, *"Therefore, do not let sin reign in your mortal body so that you obey its lusts, and do not go on presenting the members of your body to sin as instruments of unrighteousness, but present yourselves to God as those alive from the dead, and your members as instruments of righteousness to God"* (Rom 6:12,13). We are certainly to strive to obey the laws of God, knowing that we cannot do this perfectly.

Does refraining from stealing my neighbor's lawnmower qualify as a good work? A work of faith? A work of the law? It is clearly not an evil deed. It could be considered a work of the law if, by restraining my selfish desires, I think I am earning a ticket to heaven. It is not really a work of faith since it doesn't involve trusting in a promise of God.

In the early 1800's, a wave of Christian preachers began to emphasize the importance of holy living in the Christian life. Collectively, this became known as the Holiness Movement. These Protestant preachers argued that belief in God that was not reflected by a changed life, a holy life, was not true faith, and that a holy life was the real measure of whether a person was an authentic Child of God.

As acceptance grew for the notion that obedience to the law of God was the most accurate indicator of a person's faith, the feared outcome arose. Obedience to the law became the goal, pushing out other indicators of the fruits of the Spirit - love, joy, peace, patience, kindness, goodness, and gentleness. Terms such as "entire sanctification" became popular and ordinary people claimed they were living a sinless life. A Christian journal appeared called, "Guide to Christian Perfection."

Of course, no one can live a sinless life, and making this the goal distorts the purpose for which we were made, as well as causing discouragement and doubt. Jesus taught his followers that the real indicator of whether a person was a child of God was in their demonstrations of love: *"By this all men will know that you are my disciples, if you have love for one another" (Jn 13:35).*

Holy living is the natural outcome of one of the fruits of the Spirit: self-control. It is not the only fruit, nor is it the most important *("But the greatest of these is love,"* 1Cor 13:13). Our pursuit of holy living is expected, as is our pursuit of the other spiritual gifts. Holy living should never be seen as the epitome of spirituality or spiritual achievement.

I recently read a sermon written by a Protestant minister about good works. He emphatically stated that either you believe in salvation by grace through faith alone, or you believe that works somehow contribute to, or merit, your salvation. It has to be one or the other.

This is a false dichotomy. This pastor has not considered a third, valid alternative - that faith involves belief in God and trust, demonstrated through works. Salvation then depends on both an inward belief and an outward expression (works) to be validated as true faith.

I also recently heard a different Evangelical Protestant minister say to a large crowd of believers, "We [the Evangelical Protestant Church] don't have a theology of works." I would have to agree. The theology of works I grew up with was, "You should do good works because God wants you to." That was it. Disappointingly anemic, especially considering all of the rich Scripture addressing works.

The Apostle Paul tells the Ephesians that they were, "created in Christ Jesus for good works" (Eph 2:10). Good works, and works of faith, are credited to us as righteousness, since they complete our faith (James 2:21,22). With this understanding, we can rightly say that we are saved by grace, through faith (Eph 2:8), and that works are a necessary part of that faith (James 2:26).

12

Hell and Heaven

It is probably the most well-known verse in the Bible: John 3:16. Spoken by Jesus, it reads,

> *For God so loved the world that He gave His only begotten son, that whoever believes in Him will not experience eternal conscious torment, but have everlasting life.*

The Gospel in 1 verse. It rolls off most Christian's tongues without much thought, though some readers may have noticed an unfamiliar wording somewhere in the middle.

It turns out, this is not some new or archaic translation of the original Greek. Rather, I took the liberty of substituting the common teaching about Hell for the word used by Jesus to describe what happens to those who are not saved. That word is, of course, "perish." "Whoever believes in Him will not *perish*."

"Perish" is a pretty straightforward word. Ask anyone what "perish" means and you are likely to get the same answer: cease to exist, disappear, decompose into nothing. The end result is all the same. The thing that once existed, no longer exists. The Greek word for "perish" used in John 3:16 is derived from apollymi - meaning to completely destroy (Vines). Although it can also be translated "destroyed" or "lost," the most common translation of this Greek word is "perish," as in Matt 26:52, *"Then Jesus said to him, "Put your sword back in its place; for all those who take up the sword shall perish by the sword,"* and Acts 8:20, *"But Peter said to him, 'May your silver perish with you because you thought you could obtain the gift of God with money.'"* In each of these verses, perish clearly means cease to exist.

There are some who would like to make the meaning of "perish" in John 3:16 something like "be ruined" or " be condemned to hell." The problem is, this translation doesn't work for the other uses of "apollymi" in the New Testament. Looking at just the 2 verses above, we can see that ruined or condemned to hell makes no sense. Silver can't be condemned to hell. And Jesus telling Peter to put away his sword was meant to preserve his life - it didn't have anything to do with him being ruined. Perish means perish, not something else.

If this were the only passage in Scripture that told us what happened to those who are not saved, the only reasonable conclusion would be that these persons are destroyed, wiped out, made to no longer exist. Of course, it isn't the only verse. It turns out there are over 50 verses that indicate that those who are condemned at the final judgement undergo complete annihilation. God causes them to cease to exist permanently. I've listed 50 of these verse references in the Chapter Notes section at the end of this book that say this in one form or another.[1] There are others. The eternal life that is granted to those who are saved is in direct contrast to the eternal death that God bestows on those who reject Him.

If Scripture is so clear regarding the fate of the damned, how did the Church get this idea that hell is a place of never-ending physical and emotional torment? Where did this come from?

Aren't there passages that talk about hell as a fiery place of never-ending suffering?

The Greek word translated "hell" in the New Testament is "gehenna." It is used only 13 times in 5 different books - 7 times in Matthew, 3 times in Mark, and once each in Luke, James, and 2 Peter. The word "gehenna" was actually well known among the Hebrews outside of its use in Scripture since it was the name given to the trash incinerator, the burning garbage heap, outside of Jerusalem. Since there was no trash pick-up service during this time, and getting rid of trash was problematic, those in Jerusalem established a place to burn their trash outside the city walls. It is likely that the burning went on day and night given the size of the city.

When Jesus used the word "gehenna" in regards to condemned persons, listeners in the first century knew exactly what he was talking about. Those condemned would be sent to the incinerator, the place where fire consumes all. Trash did not survive gehenna. Nor would people.

Of the 13 verses that use the word "gehenna," 11 are direct quotes of Jesus. Six of these verses are when Jesus is teaching about the importance of striving for a sinless life. In a representative verse he states, *"If your right eye makes you stumble, tear it out and throw it from you; for it is better for you to lose one of the parts of your body than for your whole body to be thrown into hell"* (Mat 5:29). He goes on to repeat the exhortation noting it would be better to lose a hand or a foot than to be thrown into hell. None of these verses really tells us what hell is, although they imply that going to hell would cause us to lose our whole body, not just an important part.

Three of the verses spoken by Jesus serve as warnings of judgement for particular groups of people. In Matthew 5:22

Jesus says, *"and whoever says 'You fool' shall be guilty enough to go into the fiery hell."* Matthew 23:15 is a warning to the Scribes and Pharisees, noting that when they make a proselyte they *"make him twice as much a son of hell as yourselves."* He continues in verse 33 with the further warning, *"You serpents, you brood of vipers, how will you escape the sentence of hell."* Again, not much description about hell other than it is the place where those receiving God's harshest judgement are sent.

The verse in 2 Peter relates to sinning angels sent to hell. Apparently hell is not for humans only. James 3:6 talks about the tongue set on fire - *"the very world of iniquity."* It *"sets on fire the course of our life, and is set on fire by hell."* More fire imagery, but no descriptions about what that fire does or how long it lasts.

The last 2 verses contain some vital information. In Mat 10:28 Jesus warns,

> *"Do not fear those who kill the body but are unable to kill the soul; but rather fear Him who is able to destroy [apollymi] both soul and body in hell."*

A related verse in Luke 12:5 says, *"But I will warn you whom to fear: fear the One who, after He has killed, has authority to cast into hell; yes, I tell you, fear Him!"*

Jesus clearly states that what happens in hell is that both body and soul are destroyed. This destruction is not some sort of never ending torment. He says, *"Do not fear those who kill the body."* The phrase "kill the body" is understood by all. Life ends. Our existence on this earth ceases. Jesus says don't fear this. Rather, fear Him who has the authority to cast into hell where both body **and** soul are destroyed. By placing the phrase "kill the body" next to "kill the soul," Jesus is letting us know exactly what happens to our soul in hell. It is destroyed. It ceases to exist.

As can be seen, none of these verses say anything about never-ending suffering or eternal torment. The one passage that does give us a picture of what happens in gehenna states that both body and soul are destroyed, using the same Greek word for destroyed (apollymi) that we saw before in John 3:16.

Are there any verses in Scripture that say anything about eternal suffering in hell? Surely this common teaching has to have some biblical defense.

There are 3, maybe 4, verses that are brought up to defend an eternal conscious torment view of hell (As opposed to the 50+ verses that teach that the damned cease to exist). These verses would need to so clearly and forcefully teach eternal conscious suffering, and have no other reasonable interpretation, that they somehow negate or make us rethink our understanding of what the words "perish" and "destroyed" mean.

The first of these verses occurs in Matthew, towards the end of the book, when Jesus is teaching about what the last judgement will be like. He starts off by saying,

> *"But when the Son of Man comes in His glory, and all the angels with Him, then He will sit on His glorious throne. All the nations will be gathered before Him, and He will separate them one from another, as the shepherd separates the sheep from the goats" (25:31,32).*

After He informs the righteous that they are to inherit the kingdom, he turns to those on His left and says,

> *"Depart from Me, accursed ones, into the eternal fire which has been prepared for the devils and his*

angels" (v41).

He ends the chapter by saying,

> *"And these will go away into eternal punishment, but the righteous into eternal life."*

Most Christians have been taught for so long that hell is never-ending physical and emotional suffering that when they hear "eternal punishment," they immediately see pictures in their head of a devil with horns and a pitchfork standing over people suffering in a fiery underworld surrounded by masochistic demons.

The verse says "eternal punishment" but doesn't tell us what that punishment is. Surely the punishment is eternal, that is, it lasts forever, but the punishment could be any number of things. It could be some form of physical torture; it could be conscious separation from God; it could be forced labor; it could be a powerful ever-present depression and regret. Or, it could be the destruction of body and soul, complete and irreversible. The point is, one cannot tell what the punishment is that Jesus is talking about from this verse. Other verses are needed to inform us about what will happen to those *"accursed ones"* in hell.

Another passage that gives us a sense of what will be experienced eternally by those declared unrighteous is 2 Th 1:6,8,9:

> *For after all it is only just for God to repay with affliction those who afflict you...Dealing out retribution to those who do not know God and to those who do not obey the gospel of our Lord Jesus Christ. These will pay the penalty of eternal destruction, away from the presence of the Lord and from the glory of His power.*

So the penalty that will be handed down, the penalty experienced by those rejecting God is eternal destruction. Does the "eternal" in this verse mean that the process of destruction will go on forever, or does it mean that the end result of the destruction will last forever?

Those who argue for a hell of eternal suffering make the case for the former. But this really makes no sense. The process of destroying something goes through stages, from fully intact to completely gone. There is a time when the thing being destroyed is a fourth destroyed, one-half destroyed, and three-quarters destroyed. A person can't eternally go through a destruction - either he is moving towards total destruction which means that it will end, or the process of destruction is not progressing in which case destruction is not happening. The last phrase of the verse also points to the condemned perishing by noting eternal destruction results in being *"away from the presence of the Lord."* This would be the necessary outcome if the body and soul are both destroyed in the fire of hell.

A third verse used to support never ending suffering is Mark 9:47, the teaching of Jesus that losing an eye would be preferable to being cast into hell, "where their worm does not die, and the fire is not quenched" (v 48). A repetition of this curious verse may also follow verses 43 and 45, although the oldest Greek manuscripts do not record it there. What could *"where their worm does not die"* mean? Again, proponents of eternal suffering would say that the worm represents something that causes pain, as does the fire. Although this is one possible explanation, worms don't generally cause pain. Venomous snakes, yes. Scorpions, yes. Worms, no. Worms are God's biologic incinerator. They decompose dead things. If a bird dies and falls on the ground, it will shortly be invaded by maggots that will feed on the bird, digesting its body until it disappears. Fire, of course, will do a similar thing. Jesus gives us a picture of complete destruction by two agents that will not be stopped - undying worms and unquenchable fire. There is no language here that implies these agents fail in their task.

A fourth verse that is sometimes used to suggest never-ending suffering is Revelation 20:10. John has just seen a vision of Satan being released after a thousand years in prison. He gathers his followers for war against the saints and His holy city, but they are abruptly devoured by fire. John goes on to say, *"And the devil who deceived them was thrown into the lake of fire and brimstone, where the beast and the false prophet are also; and they will be tormented day and night forever and ever."* Later in the chapter he adds, *"And if anyone's name was not written in the book of life, he was thrown into the lake of fire"* (v15).

The phrase *"tormented day and night forever and ever"* is quite clear. It does come as a description of what John sees in a vision, however, which means it is his interpretation of what he is seeing, not a direct explanation coming from the lips of Jesus. Nevertheless, it indicates that Satan and his immediate henchmen will experience torment forever. The verse at the end of the chapter says those who are condemned will also be subject to the lake of fire. Notably, the description applied to Satan's punishment, that he *"will be tormented day and night forever and ever"* is absent. If humans are to be subjected to the same punishment as Satan, eternal torment, one would think it would be clearly stated somewhere. These verses fail to make that statement.

In summary, there are 3 or 4 verses in Scripture that, if taken in isolation, leave open the possibility of eternal conscious torment. None of them say such a thing plainly or clearly. Nowhere in Scripture are the words "eternal suffering" or "eternal torment" associated with humans condemned to hell. These verses need to be interpreted in a way that is consistent with the 50+ verses that describe the condemned as those that "perish," are "destroyed," and "are no more."

The teaching of hell as a place of never ending suffering is so pervasive in the church today that changing this error will take decades of concerted effort. Most of the passages referred to above are simple and clear. Despite all the biblical evidence, many will continue to have objections. I will address 2 common ones now.

Objection 1: Causing permanent destruction of both body and soul is not an adequate penalty for rejecting God. Only eternal suffering can pay for this sin.

Answer: God is a God of justice. He is also a God of love and mercy. Determining the penalty for any sin is for God alone to decide. He defines justice. Any opinion from any human regarding what is the right penalty for rejecting God is only that - an opinion. The appropriate penalty, God's judgement, must be understood from what is written in Scripture. There is no other source to gain this understanding.

The idea that God would subject creatures that He created to eternal suffering is inconsistent with Scriptures' representation of His character. He can bring judgement on sin swiftly and severely, but this judgement never goes beyond ending the life of the condemned. Sodom and Gomorrah are destroyed by fire for their corporate sin. Their lives are forfeited in a few hours. The humans living at the time of Noah are lost by drowning, also likely occurring over hours. Ananias and Sapphira are struck down in an instant for their lies to the Apostles. Never does God advocate or hand down a penalty of prolonged torture for any sin. Such morally repugnant behavior is a manifestation of evil lurking in humans, not a characteristic of a perfectly just, perfectly loving, perfectly merciful God.

Eternal destruction, that is, the permanent and complete removal of a person's body, soul and spirit from the realm of God, is the judgement that most fits our human understanding of justice, love and mercy in combination. The wages of sin is death. Those whose sins are never covered by the blood of Christ will experience death - eternal and absolute. While God does tell us that these persons will go through a period of "weeping and gnashing of teeth" - severe emotional distress once they have realized they have forfeited eternal paradise - this period of distress will end with their incineration in gehenna. A merciful end to a rebellious life.

Objection 2: Since human souls are inherently immortal, everyone will live forever, either in heaven or hell.

Answer: The idea that bodies are mortal and souls are immortal really comes from ancient Egyptian and Greek philosophy. Roughly 4 centuries before Jesus was born, Plato solidified the concept of an immortal soul, writing in The Phaedo: "The soul, whose inseparable attribute is life, will never admit life's opposite, death. Thus the soul is shown to be immortal, and since immortal, indestructible." Unfortunately, the Church in large part adopted this understanding from its earliest days.

The Bible teaches something very different. Eternal life is a gift given by God to those whose name is written in the Book of Life. John 3:16 attests to this. It makes no sense for God to reward people with eternal life if they already have eternal life. The Apostle Paul proclaims that when Christ returns to claim those that are His, *"the dead will be raised imperishable, and we will be changed. For this perishable must put on the imperishable, and this mortal must put on immortality."* (1 Cor 15:52,53) There would be no need to "put on" immortality if we were already immortal.

God created life: body and soul. God alone is inherently immortal. He has chosen to rescue a group of people, those who love Him, from their merited destination of eternal death. Praise be to God!

Heaven

What happens to people when they die? Are the saved immediately whisked away to heaven, and the lost to hell? Is there an in-between time? What about Purgatory? And what is heaven really going to be like? In order to answer these questions, one final biblical survey is in order.

The word "heaven" occurs 456 times in the Old and New Testaments. It has four very distinct meanings. The first is the physical space above our heads. This is the most common usage. Passages often include "heaven" and "earth" (103x) to indicate the whole universe. Other verses use the phrases "under heaven," or "heaven above," or "from heaven" (~200x) to indicate the place where something is or from whence something comes.

The second usage indicates the place where God currently resides, as in Deut 26:15, *"Look down from Your holy habitation, from heaven, and bless Your people Israel ..."* This place is often imagined as somewhere above us, but not always. Jesus now also resides in this place with the Father: *"For Christ did not enter into a holy place made with hands, a mere copy of the true one, but into heaven itself, now to appear in the presence of God for us"* (Heb 9:24). Angels and other beings also inhabit this realm: *"But even if we, or an angel from heaven, should preach to you a gospel contrary to what we have preached to you, he is to be accursed"* (Gal 1:8). This use occurs about 100 times.

The third use is in the phrase "kingdom of heaven." Jesus uses this phrase 38 times in the book of Matthew; John the Baptist uses it once. It occurs nowhere else. In preparing the people for Jesus' ministry, John the Baptist proclaims, *"Repent for the kingdom of heaven is at hand"* (Mat 3:2). Jesus uses many analogies to describe what the kingdom is like: a sower of seed; a mustard seed; a fishing net; a pearl; like yeast. The kingdom of heaven is God's holy realm that includes those people who have accepted the truth that Jesus is the Messiah and who humbly and sacrificially live out their faith (Mat 5:3 and 10, Mat 18:3,4).

The fourth use of "heaven" occurs only twice: *"But according to His promise we are looking for new heavens and a new earth, in which righteousness dwells,"* (1Pet 3:13) and, *"Then I saw a new heaven and a new earth, for the first heaven and the first earth passed away, and there is no longer any sea"* (Rev 21:1).

This "new heaven" was in the vision given to John about what will happen after the final judgement. It seems that when Jesus returns, he will recreate the current earth and heaven as the place we will live. The "new heaven" will replace the "first heaven." We are not given a description of what this new heaven will be like, but given that it will replace the first heaven, it will likely represent all that space above the new earth. Whether it will contain stars, or other heavenly bodies is not known. It won't contain a sun as God will provide the light and energy needed for our existence (Rev 22:5). The first earth and heaven will be destroyed by fire, or some energy appearing as fire (2Pet 3:10).

The remarkable thing about these 4 different meanings of the word "heaven" is that none of them represent how the word is used today. Over 400 verses, and none use the word to mean the place we will spend eternity! The new heaven is not where we will live. We will live on the new earth, which will also be the new home of God (Rev 21:3). God's current abode, heaven, will cease to exist, or will become one with the new earth, since He will then live among us (Rev 22:1).

What will our eternal existence be like on this new earth? It certainly won't include people with wings, prancing among the clouds, playing harps all day. The popular media are so wrong when it comes to depicting "heaven" that it is a scandal, really. Descriptions of this new earth in Scripture include well developed cities, rivers, trees, and lush gardens (Is 51:3, Ez 36:35, Is 55:13). The capitol city, New Jerusalem, will be gorgeous, with a wall made of precious stones and streets shining with gold (Rev 21:10-27). There will be no more death, disease, or corruption. Just as our bodies will have been remade into recognizable but perfect biological machines, so too the earth will be remade into a recognizable but perfect place to live.

What will we do for eternity? We will do the will of God. That will has always included constructive work, meaningful relationships, enjoyment of God's creation, and heartfelt worship. We will sing, dance, play, eat, and laugh.[2]

This new heaven and new earth will be given to the Children of God after the resurrection of mankind and the judgement. Before that happens, between our death and the settlement of this new earth, what happens? Are we conscious of our surroundings? And what about those destined for eternal destruction?

There are 2 prevailing teachings in the Christian Church describing that in-between period of time. One group teaches that we will experience a "soul sleep," a time when our spirits/souls are kept by God in a state of unconscious, but peaceful existence, awaiting Christ's return to earth. The other teaching is what I will call "soul awake." In this scenario, the spirits of the Children of God are transported to heaven to exist with God the Father and Son, awaiting the return of Christ to the earth. The spirits of the unrighteous will exist in a bleak, dreadful state, in a place called Hades, separated from God, awaiting their final sentence. There are some variations, but these are the basic explanations.

So which is it? Growing up I was taught the "soul sleep" paradigm, in spite of Jesus' proclamation to the thief during the crucifixion, and didn't really question it until writing this book.

It is easy to see where the "soul sleep" idea comes from. Jesus uses the picture of sleeping to describe the state of the dead throughout his ministry. In John 11, Jesus is being beckoned to attend Lazarus who is very sick. After a two day delay, Jesus says to His disciples, *"Our friend Lazarus has fallen asleep; but I go, so that I may awaken him out of sleep"* (v 11). His disciples think he is being literal and respond, *"Lord, if he has fallen asleep, he will recover"* (v 12). The narrative continues letting us know what is really going on: *"Now Jesus had spoken of his death, but they thought he was speaking of a literal sleep. So Jesus said to them plainly, 'Lazarus is dead'"* (v 13,14).

In Matthew 9, we are told of a synagogue official who comes to Jesus after his daughter has died. He pleads with Jesus to come to lay His hand on her. Jesus follows the man to his house and upon entering and seeing the mourners says, *"Leave, for the girl has not died but is asleep."* They began laughing at Him. But when the crowd had been sent out, He entered and took her by the hand, and the girl got up (v 24,25).

Both Luke and Paul follow suit by using the "sleep" terminology to refer to death. Luke says of Stephen as he is being stoned, *"Then falling on his knees, he cried out in a loud voice, 'Lord, do not hold this sin against them.' Having said this, he fell asleep"* (Acts 7:60). Speaking of King David he says, *"For David, after he had served the purpose of God in his own generation, fell asleep, and was laid among his fathers and underwent decay"* (Acts 13:36). Paul tells the Corinthians, *"After that He [Jesus] appeared to more than 500 brethren at one time, most of whom remain until now, but some have fallen asleep"* (1Cor 15:6). He teaches the Thessalonians: *"But we do not want you to be uninformed, brethren, about those who have fallen asleep, so that you will not grieve as those who have no hope"* (1Th 4:13).

"Asleep" is the dominant descriptor used in reference to Christians who have died. It is certainly understandable how some conclude that when Christians die, they enter a sleep state - one where our spirit and soul are not fully conscious, but kept by God, safe and sound, waiting for His return. There are other verses, however, that indicate we are aware and conscious after death. These need to be understood in a way that is consistent with the sleep language used throughout the New Testament.

The most compelling verse is likely Jesus's words to the thief on the cross. Jesus answers him after his plea to be remembered *"when you come in your Kingdom," "Truly I say to you, today you will be with me in Paradise"* (Luk 23:43). This clear promise of a relationship immediately after death speaks to a conscious existence. We know that Jesus went to the Father in heaven after death. Jesus tells the thief he will be there too. It's a bit hard to imagine Jesus was saying "I will care for your spirit in Paradise while you sleep, and someday I will awaken you to everlasting life." The natural meaning the thief would understand was that after death, on that day, he would be with Jesus, aware of his surroundings, in Paradise.

The Apostle Paul tells the Corinthians, *"We are of good courage, I say, and prefer rather to be absent from the body, and to be at home with our Lord"* (1Cor 5:8). Paul is confident that when his spirit leaves his body, it will be present with the Lord. He repeats this in Philippians 1, *"For I am hard pressed from both directions, having the desire to depart and be with Christ, for that is very much better"* (v 23). Again, it wouldn't make much sense to be present and not know it. He says, *"at home with our Lord."* That would be in heaven with Jesus, basking in His love.

Moses and Elijah appeared with Jesus during His transfiguration (Mat 17:1-3). These men had been dead for 100's of years. Their bodies lay in the ground, decayed. Yet they appear with Jesus, talking with Him, clearly not in a state of spiritual slumber. At the end of his earthly life, we are told that Elijah, *"went up by a whirlwind into heaven"* (2Ki 2:11). In Revelation, John gives us glimpses of what is happening in the heavenly realm. There, he sees the saints, not sleeping, but calling out to God to hasten His judgement on the earth (Rev 6:10).

All of these verses tell us that when we die, if we are in Christ, our spirit heads to heaven to be with Jesus. Those that are not in Christ will be thrown into Hades (Mat 11:23, Luk 16:23), where there will be weeping and gnashing of teeth (Luk 13:28), to await the final judgement.

If this is indeed true, then why would Jesus refer to the dead as "asleep?"

Sleeping bodies can look dead - motionless, lifeless. Someone who is asleep is, of course, not dead. Their brains continue to function. They dream, they can react to pain, their subconscience can process information. We generally cannot see that. To us, a sleeping person can just look dead. But to Jesus, the dead person is just asleep. He can see their spirit, which has left the body. He can wake them up. Though the body is lifeless, the spirit is alive. Referring to the dead as "asleep" was one more way that Jesus asserted His authority over death.

Finally, what of Purgatory? The Catholic Church teaches that certain believers who die in Christ, must undergo a period of cleansing, or purification, before entering heaven. In the words of the Catholic Catechism:

> All who die in God's grace and friendship, but still imperfectly purified, are indeed assured of their eternal salvation; but after death they undergo purification, so as to achieve the holiness necessary to enter the joy of heaven.[3]

This doctrine of "final purification" is also held by the Orthodox Church, although they do not call it Purgatory, a term that suggests suffering. The Orthodox Church's version of this final purification is less about suffering and more about maturing each soul to a state of perfection, thus achieving full divinization.

For most Protestants, the idea that believers would need to undergo some sort of final purification is difficult to grasp. Since the prevailing view is that all sin, past, present and future, is forgiven at conversion, and the slate is wiped clean forever, the Child of God is ready to enter heaven immediately. To suggest that such souls need some further cleansing, would be considered against biblical teaching.

So, what does the Bible say about purification, and how did the Catholic Church arrive at this doctrine? A quick search of Scripture reveals that the word "Purgatory" does not occur in either the Old or New Testaments. Neither does the word penance. There is no mention of any "purification" after death, nor is the term "divinization" found.

The need for a period of final purification stems from the Catholic Church's teaching regarding sin and its consequences. Over the centuries, various ideas were developed by church leaders to explain the effect sin has on our soul, our body, and our righteousness. The severity of sin was divided into two categories, venial sin (considered minor) and mortal sin (that deserving of damnation). Lumping murder as a sin on the same level as losing patience with your mother didn't seem to make much sense. Likewise, the type of punishment that these sins merited would not be the same. Punishment was further divided into two types, temporal and eternal. Eternal punishment was hell. Temporal punishment was that act of penance that the Church deemed necessary to demonstrate repentance and contrition for a particular sin.

Considering this hierarchy of sin, the Catholic Church came to the conclusion that persons who commit a mortal sin have separated themselves from God to such a degree that only repentance and penance can bring them back into a relationship with the Body of Christ. That is, a serious sin demonstrates that the Spirit of God is not abiding in a person, and thus they are not saved. They are headed for eternal punishment. Venial sins need to be confessed, and an appropriate temporal punishment applied, but these sins do not put one in danger of eternal punishment. Those minor sins that are not confessed, or those for which temporal punishment has not been experienced, will need to be dealt with after death - Purgatory.

Unfortunately, there are multiple problems with this doctrine. First, Scripture never differentiates between those sins that separate us from God and those that do not. ALL sin separates us from God. The Apostle Paul says *"all have sinned and fall short of the glory of God"* (Rom 3:23). And he clearly states that *"the wages of sin is death"* (Rom 6:23). There is no differentiation between minor and major sin. In fact, James drives this home by saying, *"For whoever keeps the whole law and yet stumbles in one point, he has become guilty of all"* (Jas 2:10). Losing patience with my mom makes me guilty of the whole law. Losing patience with my mom is actually a mortal sin, one that deserves eternal punishment, and will result in eternal punishment without the forgiveness that comes through faith in Christ.

The second problem is that of "temporal punishment." Christ took on the punishment for my sin. Period. That is the essence of the Gospel! Saying that Jesus suffered on the cross in my place, for my eternal punishment, but not for my temporal punishment makes little sense. Yes, it is true that sin has consequences. If I get drunk and accidentally kill someone in my car, I will likely spend time in jail. That is a civil penalty handed down by the government in order to recognize the wrong I have committed. It is not a punishment that somehow restores my relationship with God. The Children of God are never punished for their sin. They are disciplined, which can be painful, but never punished. Discipline is a loving action taken by God during our lifetime to guide us back onto the narrow path (Heb 12:10).

Access to heaven is only granted to those attaining full and complete righteousness. Humans can never earn or attain this righteousness by keeping the law. Nor can they attain this by performing some sort of penance or accepting some punishment. This righteousness can only come by faith in Jesus as our Lord and Savior. *"The blood of Jesus cleanses us from all sin"* (1Jn 1:7), that's both minor and major sin. That cleansing is complete. For the church to teach that we must go through a period of unpleasant purification after death to "achieve the holiness necessary to enter the joy of heaven," means that

Christ's suffering on the cross was **not** sufficient to bring us into glory. Must we suffer too? No, praise God, we have been freed from the penalty of sin: *"The free gift of God is eternal life"* (Rom 6:23). "Free" would not include a required period of penance or suffering.

Jesus told the thief on the cross, *"Today you will be with me in Paradise."* There would be no period of purification after death for this sinner. No penance to pay for his unconfessed sin. His faith in Jesus was credited as righteousness. All members of the Body of Christ will see the face of their Redeemer, and experience His Divine love, on the day of their death. To God be the Glory. Amen.

13

A Roadmap to Reunification

I often see patients in my clinic who are quite overweight. I try not to ignore the health ramifications of this problem and will typically ask them if they would like to lose weight. They all say, "Yes!" I then ask them what they would be willing to give up in order to lose weight. Their enthusiasm begins to wane. I ask about sugary drinks. "Would you be willing to give up sweet tea and soda?" Most say yes with some hesitation. "What about fast food?" At this point the uncomfortable body language begins to show, along with explanations about how they don't eat it that often, and sometimes they just don't have time to cook. If I talk about decreasing the amount of meat they eat or discuss the fact they should be eating mostly veggies, whole grains, and fruit, I've lost most of them. The food that I am asking them to give up is neither essential, nor is some of it even healthy, but they have become so used to eating in a certain way, that thinking about making some changes becomes unthinkable.

In order for the Christian Church on earth to reunify, each group, Catholic, Orthodox, and Protestant, will need to give up a few things. These things are teachings that are neither essential, nor are some of them even healthy. The changes that I outline below wouldn't solve every misunderstanding or disagreement, but would go a long way to fostering the unity that Jesus fervently prayed for prior to His glorification.

In regards to works, the Protestant Church needs give up its teaching that works are not a part of faith. It needs to acknowledge that the Bible teaches an intimate connection between faith and works. Specifically, the church needs to accept the biblical teaching of forgiveness being granted through works of faith such as prayer, confession, and baptism. It also needs to accept that we will be judged based on our works, and that good works and works of faith are essential for salvation as they complete, or perfect, our faith.

The Catholic and Orthodox Churches need to drop any talk of merit in association with salvation. Humans cannot merit any part of the righteousness that is required for entry into God's kingdom. Even using language that tries to link our "merit" with Christ working in us, creates a sense of duality - our salvation becomes a joint venture, with Christ doing some of the work and humans doing some of the work. We do not work our way into heaven. Our salvation is due to the work of God alone, Father, Son, and Holy Spirit.

In regards to the Lord's Supper, both Catholic and Orthodox Churches need to stop teaching that this celebration is a sacrifice, or a "re-presentation" of a sacrifice. Jesus's sacrifice on the cross was done once for all sin and for all time. Taking part in the Lord's Supper and hearing a priest declare that the "sacrifice" of Christ, that is, His body and blood, are being presented to Christ, is confusing and misleading. It causes the communicant to think that this re-presentation of the "sacrifice" is needed to atone for their sin. Nothing could be further from the truth.

Protestant Churches need to stop teaching that the Lord's Supper and baptism are merely symbolic acts, without any direct spiritual benefit. The forgiveness that only comes through faith in Christ is conferred to those who participate in baptism, trusting in His promise. The body and blood of Christ are truly present in the bread and the wine, nourishing our souls as the visible elements nourish our body. These supernatural occurrences are part of our faith. They are part of the Mystery of God's provision for His Children, the Body of Christ. Teachings that deny that these benefits are conferred by faithful participation, eviscerate God's prescribed methods for equipping His chosen people.

In regards to Purgatory, the Catholic Church needs to amend their teaching on final purification. The blood of Christ is the basis for our final purification. There is no penance or suffering that is due to pay for or achieve the holiness required of God. The Orthodox Church needs to amend its teaching on divinization. Humans do not become Gods (the doctrine of Theosis). God adopts us into His family; He makes us brothers and sisters to Christ; and He makes us like Christ in clothing us with complete righteousness. We are neither made equal to God, nor are we made into a God.

The various Protestant denominations need to stop using niche teachings about behaviors as an indicator of our membership in the Body of Christ. Specifically, teachings about what we wear, when and how we worship, the drinking of alcohol containing beverages, and the use of dance and music for worship and celebration should never be used to judge our belonging to Christ. These activities may be practiced in ways that raise concern about the state of our heart, but they are a matter of Christian freedom that should only be called into question when they bring dishonor to God.

A person's commitment to achieving an outcome can be gauged by what they are willing to give up to make it happen. The same is true for any organization. Jesus prayed for His Church, *"The glory which You have given Me I have given to them, that they may be one, just as We are one; I in them and You in Me, that they may be perfected in unity, so that the world may know that you sent Me, and loved them, even as You have loved Me"* (Jn 17:22,23).

"Perfected in unity." How important do we think this is to God? Are we willing to give up some of our non-essential teachings for the sake of unity? I'm afraid for many Christians, and Christian churches, the answer is "No." Christian unity falls low on the list of priorities, certainly below preserving the status quo and remaining comfortable with what we were taught as children.

It is time to put aside our comfort, to roll up our sleeves, and to reconstitute the Body of Christ into a unified whole. This needs to be done not only for our sakes, but for the sake of the world.

Chapter Notes

Chapter 3

1. See http://www.todayifoundout.com/index.php/2013/09/george-washington-never-chopped-down-a-cherry-tree/, last accessed 10/11/2017.

2. See http://www.mountvernon.org/digital-encyclopedia/article/cherry-tree-myth/, last accessed 10/11/2017

3. Taking into consideration every science experiment ever done, in all of human history, not one human neuron cell has ever emerged from the mixing together of the right atoms in the right proportions. Accordingly, not one random connection between neurons has ever been made in this manner. The brain contains 100 trillion connections, each one providing part of a complex set of inputs that makes human functioning possible. Science in no way supports Darwinian evolution.

4. See https://www.allaboutarchaeology.org/hittite-faq.htm, last accessed 10/10/2017.

5. See https://www.haaretz.com/jewish/archaeology/.premium-1.652843, last accessed 10/11/2017.

6. See http://www.nytimes.com/1990/02/22/world/believers-score-in-battle-over-the-battle-of-jericho.html, last accessed 10/10/2017.

7. RL Hipkins, and KL Thompson, "Kaibab Formation," in Grand Canyon Geology, 2nd ed. (New York: Oxford University

CHAPTER NOTES

Press, 2003), pp 196-211. And many others showing marine fossils far removed from current oceans.

8. See 100 Prophecies: Ancient Biblical prophecies that foretold the future by G. Konig (CreateSpace Independent Publishing Platform, Oct 2008).

Chapter 4

1. See http://www.theopedia.com/marcionism, last accessed 10/11/2017.

2. See https://en.wikipedia.org/wiki/Shabbat, last accessed 10/11/2017.

Chapter 5

1. See www.geocentrism.com or www.geocenticity.com.

2. For a rather compelling look at these time periods, written by a physicist, see God and Science, Gerald Schroeder, PhD (Free Press, June 16, 2009).

Chapter 6

1. Both Mormons and Jehovah's Witnesses believe that Jesus is not equal to God the Father. Jehovah's Witnesses believe Jesus became the Messiah at His baptism. Mormons believe Jesus is just one of an enormous number of demigods. See http://www.christiananswers.net/q-eden/edn-r005.html, and https://www.thegospelcoalition.org/article/9-things-you-should-know-about-mormonism.

Chapter 7

1. For a more complete review of these verses see <u>Baptism, A Biblical Study</u> by Jack Cottrell (College Press Publishing, 2002).

2. To read an Evangelical Protestant's strong view on baptism and the Body, see <u>The Baptized Body</u> by Peter Leithart (CanonPress, 2007).

Chapter 8

1. See http://www.anabaptists.org/history/the-schleitheim-confession.html, last accessed 10/15/2017.

2. The story of the Chinese General is thought to be fiction by some, See https://en.wikipedia.org/wiki/Feng_Yuxiang, last accessed 10/15/2017, but the practice still exists today, http://www.washingtonpost.com/wp-dyn/content/article/2007/08/26/AR2007082601278.html, last accessed 10/15/2017.

3. Luther struggled with this inconsistency - salvation by grace through faith, and the salvation of infants. He resolved this by stating that baptism "worked faith in the infant," see https://www.lcms.org/about/beliefs/faqs/doctrine, last accessed 10/15/17. This explanation cannot be rationally defended, nor is there any indication in Scripture that infants can have faith. The jumping of John in Elizabeth's womb does prove that the Spirit can have effects on infants, but does not speak to any sort of faith, at least not the kind that Scripture refers to.

4. Besides the verses in Psalm 51 and Rom 3, there are also: 2Chr 29:24, Ezr 6:17, Eze 45:22, Rom 5:12, Rom 7:14, Gal 3:22, 1Jn 1:8.

CHAPTER NOTES

5. To be fair to those who are Reformed, the Reformed church does say that apostasy happens. But, they define apostasy as falling away from the church, little "c," not from the Church, capital "C." This means that to the Reformed, apostasy is having a falling out from your local church, not from God. They would say that anyone who appears to have fallen away from the Body of Christ, never really belonged in the first place. Thus their difficulty with "we were all baptized into one body."

Chapter 9

1. Catechism of the Catholic Church, p384 (First Image Books, 1995).

2. See http://www.utm.edu/staff/caldwell/bfm/2000/7.html, last accessed 10/15/2017.

3. See https://www.iclnet.org/pub/resources/text/wittenberg/luther/catechism/web/cat-14.html, last accessed 10/15/17.

4. See https://soundfaith.com/sermons/50050-a-catechism-for-use-of-the-people-called-methodists, last accessed 10/15/2017.

5. See http://www.reformed.org/documents/wcf_with_proofs/, last accessed 10/15/2017.

Chapter 10

1. See https://www.catholicity.com/prayer/prayers.html, last accessed 10/15/2017.

2. See http://www.ourcatholicprayers.com/prayers-to-st-gerard.html, last accessed 10/15/2017.

3. See http://saintbenedictprotection.com/saint-benedict-prayers/, last accessed 10/15/2017.

4. See http://www.dictionary.com/browse/prayer, last accessed 10/15/2017.

Chapter 11

1. I borrowed this analogy from C.S. Lewis – not sure of the exact reference. My wife mentioned it to me about the time I was writing this chapter.

1. Catechism of the Catholic Church, p535-36 (First Image Books, 1995).

2. Ibid., p 541-42.

Chapter 12

1. Ps 9:3, 9:5, 9:6, 21:9, 36:12, 48:12, 48:14, 49:20, 52:5, 59:13, 73:18, 73:19, 73:27, 92:7, 92:9; Pr 2:22, 10:25, 12:7, 24:20; Ps 34:16, 37:9, 10, 20, 22, 28, 36, 38, 50:22, 58:8, 145:20, 1:4, 1:6, 2:12; Is 33:11, 12, 51:8; Mal 4:3; Mat 3:10, 7:13; Gal 6:8; 1Cor 3:17; Rom 2:12; Phi 1:28, 3:19; Heb 6:8, 10:39, 12:29; Ja 4:12; Acts 3:23; 2Pet 2:1, 12, 3:7, 9; Rev 11:18.

2. For a wonderful description of what life will be like on the new earth, See Heaven by Randy Alcorn (Tyndale House Publishers, October 2004).

3. Catechism of the Catholic Church, p291 (First Image Books, 1995)

CHAPTER NOTES

ABOUT THE AUTHOR

Paul Dassow, MD, MSPH, is a physician, medical educator, medical researcher, and disciple of Jesus Christ. He currently resides with his wife of 29 years on Lookout Mountain in Tennessee. They have 6 children.

Dr. Dassow's professional interests include obstetrics, healthy aging, and global health. He takes medical teams into Haiti at least once per year and is pictured on the back cover bonding with one of his diminutive patients.